AQA PSYCHOLOGY
A LEVEL PAPER THREE

FORENSIC PSYCHOLOGY

The *Extending Knowledge and Skills* series is a fresh approach to A Level Psychology, designed for the greater demands of the new AQA specification and assessment, and especially written to stretch and challenge students aiming for higher grades.

Dealing with the AQA's **Paper 3: Forensic Psychology**, this book is deliberately laid out with the assessment objectives in mind, from **AO1: Knowledge and understanding material**, followed by **AO2: Application material**, to **AO3: Evaluation and analysis material**. Providing the most in-depth, accessible coverage available of individual topics in Paper 3, the text is packed full of pedagogical features, including:

- **Question time** features to ensure that the reader is consistently challenged throughout the book.
- **New research** sections clearly distinguished within each chapter to ensure readers have access to the most cutting-edge material.
- A clear focus on the **assessment objectives** for the Paper topic to ensure readers know when and where to apply knowledge.
- The use of **example answers with examiner-style comments** to provide greater insight into how to/how not to answer exam questions.

An engaging, relevant and challenging text that broadens student understanding beyond that of the average textbook, this is the essential companion for any student taking the AQA A Level Paper 3 in Psychology.

Phil Gorman is an experienced psychology teacher and Assistant Principal Examiner for Paper 3 of the AQA A Level Psychology specification. He has been teaching this subject at A Level for over 25 years and examining for roughly the same amount of time. His examining experience has (in the past) taken him to the position of Chief Examiner for Edexcel A Level Psychology.

Extending Knowledge and Skills

The *Extending Knowledge and Skills Series* is a fresh approach to A Level psychology, designed for greater demands of the new AQA specification and assessment, and especially written to stretch and challenge students aiming for higher grades.

Going beyond the reach of traditional revision textbooks, each book in the series provides wider explanations and greater levels of detail on each of the main topics within each paper option and shows how to apply this knowledge in an exam setting to produce higher tier responses.

Books in the Series:

AQA Psychology A Level Paper Three

Forensic Psychology

Phil Gorman

Routledge
Taylor & Francis Group

LONDON AND NEW YORK

First published 2021
by Routledge
2 Park Square, Milton Park, Abingdon, Oxon OX14 4RN

and by Routledge
52 Vanderbilt Avenue, New York, NY 10017

Routledge is an imprint of the Taylor & Francis Group, an informa business

British Library Cataloguing-in-Publication Data
A catalogue record for this book is available from the British Library

Library of Congress Cataloging-in-Publication Data
A catalog record has been requested for this book

ISBN: 978 03674 0393 5 (hbk)
ISBN: 978 03674 0394 2 (pbk)
ISBN: 978 04293 5584 4 (ebk)

Typeset in Goudy Old Style and Frutiger
by Servis Filmsetting Ltd, Stockport, Cheshire

I would like to thank all the fantastic individuals I have worked with over the course of my career. I have benefited from all your enthusiasm, encouragement and wisdom. To anyone I have worked with who doesn't fall into that category, I would like to say, 'don't worry, I've forgotten you already'.

Contents

Illustrations

Tables

Chapter 1
Introduction

The aims of this book

This book is intended for A Level Psychology students studying the AQA syllabus and has been developed in order to provide further elaboration for the main Paper 3 topics. This particular book will deal with the optional topic of Forensic Psychology from section D of Paper 3.

The book has been deliberately laid out with the assessment objectives in mind, so you will find AO1 – Knowledge and understanding material first, followed by AO2 – Application material and then AO3 – Evaluation and analysis material.

Each of the assessment objectives will have an injunction/command word or some other indication that will give you an idea of the particular objective being assessed and how you are supposed to answer the question.

AO1 will include some of the following injunctions/commands words that will indicate you are required to show knowledge and understanding:

Compare – Identify similarities and differences.
Identify – Name or state what it is.
Name – Identify using a technical term.
Describe – Provide an account of.
Distinguish – Explain how two things differ.
Explain – Show what the purpose or reason for something is.
Give – Provide an answer from memory or from the information shown.
Outline – Provide the main characteristics.
State – Clearly set out.
What is meant by – Provide a definition.

AO2 will open with some kind of stem, which might be in the form of some information that you will need to refer to in your answer. For example:

Question 1

In the past, the assumption has been made that offender profiling is only applicable to crimes, such as serial murder or sex crimes. However, in recent years it has started to be used for a range of other crimes, such as arson, burglary and even terror offences.

With reference to the top-down and bottom-up approach to profiling, explain why profiling may have only been seen to be useful for certain crimes in the past but is now seen to be relevant to a wider range of crimes?

Alternatively, AO2 questions may provide a description of a scenario with the names of some fictional character(s) who are involved in a situation that is relevant to an area of psychology. You could then be asked to explain this situation using knowledge derived from the relevant topic.

Question 2

Kris is a very active person who is always on the lookout for new activities he can get involved in because he gets really bored by just sitting at home watching TV. Jay, on the other hand, is quite happy to stay at home and read a good book; he doesn't need a lot of action in his life, as he gets quite enough stimulation at home.

Using Eysenck's theory, explain which one out of Kris and Jay is more likely to become involved in crime and why?

Questions with a stem like this, which then ask you to refer to the stem in some way, are looking to assess AO2, so you need to ensure that you make clear reference to the stem by using some of the information as part of your answer. You will see examples of these in the coming chapters with some sample answers to show you how to deal with them.

AO3 will include some of the following injunctions/commands words that will indicate you are required to demonstrate skills of analysis and evaluation.

Discuss – Present strengths and weaknesses of a topic (in 16-mark questions, this can also require some element of description and can be taken as similar to describe and evaluate).

Evaluate – Make a judgement about a topic with reference to evidence.

One of the important features of this book and other books in the series is that there is a clear emphasis on the kind of skills required for the A Level Psychology exam, so the plenary sections use questions that are focused on exam skills and, at the end of every chapter, there are some exam style questions with advice on how to answer them and examples of the kinds of answers that could be given to gain very high marks. Key words will be presented in bold and placed in a glossary at the end of each chapter, to make it easier to follow what these words mean and be able to use them more readily yourself.

Further features include an emphasis on new research that is both up to date and challenging, so there will be topics that don't just follow the usual pattern but will make you think again about the kinds of topics that you are studying.

The book also uses the technique of interleaving by bringing back topics from earlier studies to reinforce and consolidate earlier learning. All too often, topics that have been studied earlier can be forgotten and it has been show that by regularly revisiting these topics, it is possible to remember much more easily than by simply trying to cram them all in at the end.

What is a crime?

In the past, the forensic psychology topic had a section concerned with the definition of crime, but this was removed to make the topic less content heavy and to make it more in line with other topics in this section. However, it is still worth considering what we are talking about when assessing if some behaviour can be defined as criminal or not. Although forensic psychology covers more than just the psychology of crime, it still makes up a major part of what needs to be studied in this section.

Activity 1

Look at the list of behaviours identified below and for each one decide whether it is a crime or not, then try to explain why it may, or may not, be considered a crime.

Example of behaviour	Crime Y/N	Reasons why it may be a crime	Reasons why it may not be a crime
Taking drugs			
Public nudity			
Damaging property			
Theft			
Adultery			
Hitting a child			
Killing someone			

A simple definition of crime could be, anything that goes against the law of the land, which makes it easy in some respects, as you could then simply say that if there is a law that says you shouldn't do something and you do it, then that's a crime. However, as with most things in life (and definitely in psychology), simple ideas are not always as useful as they first appear and there are a number of factors to be considered in whether or not we can say that something is a crime. Other definitions of crime might include a moral question of whether an act is not just illegal but is immoral too, so we could say that a crime is anything that goes against the moral values of society, whatever they are!

1. The law changes over time – what was considered illegal in the past might not be any more and what was once legal might not be now, e.g. in the past in the UK it was illegal to be gay but legal to beat your children; some strange morals in play there.

2. Moral values vary between people – from the two examples above, we can see that people can have different views on what is right and wrong and it's difficult to have an absolute view of what is and is not immoral. Even if we take the most extreme example of killing someone (which everyone would agree is bad) then there can still be different views about in what circumstances it might be OK to take someone's life, e.g. is it OK to kill someone if they have taken someone else's life? Is it OK to kill someone when you're at war with them? Who decides when it's OK or not?

3. Cultural differences in morality – different societies have different ideas about what's right and wrong. This suggests that what we view as right and wrong isn't innate, coming from some form of universal conscience that we are all born with. Culture is based on what we learn as we grow and develop, learning the norms and values (in this case morals) of our society and they are sometimes quite different from one another, e.g. in the UK the use of certain recreational drugs is illegal but not in other countries and yet the consumption of alcohol is legal but not so in other societies. Many of these differences seem contradictory and sometimes crazy but are justified in the context of the particular culture in which they occur.

4. Specific circumstances – most countries around the world have some process for making a judgement about the specific circumstances in which a behaviour occurs and most courts will make a judgement based on these rather than simply taking an absolutist view (that any behaviour that goes against the law is criminal regardless of the specific circumstances). Examples can include issues such as self-defence, in the context of killing someone, but can also be more day-to-day when considering issues such as public nudity.

Think!

Can you think of any other examples of behaviour where the specific circumstances would need to be considered before deciding whether an act is illegal or not?

What is covered in the Forensic Psychology topic?

The topic considers three main questions:

- How do we distinguish a criminal from the rest of the population?
- What makes someone turn to crime?
- What should we do with criminals?

These three questions are developed by looking at **offender profiling**, the **biological and psychological explanations of offending behaviour** and **dealing with offending behaviour**. These are clearly very important areas of investigation for society, as well as for psychologists.

The first of these areas to be developed, **offender profiling**, considers the attempts made to identify a criminal in a situation where there are few conventional clues as to the identity of the perpetrator and we need some way of narrowing down the possible pool of suspects. This is particularly true when faced with very serious crimes, such as murder and rape, and even more so when there is clear evidence that such a person is going to do it repeatedly.

In the absence of evidence from eyewitnesses or other identification methods such as CCTV, traditional police work will use physical evidence from the crime scene such as fingerprints and, increasingly these days, DNA. However, in the absence of such evidence, psychological profilers will try to use behavioural evidence from the crime scene in order to come up with an idea about the personality, social situation and possibly even location of the offender.

This area of psychology is one that has received a lot of focus in the entertainment media in which the profiler is portrayed as possessing amazing mental powers in figuring out the identity of suspects in books and TV shows such as *Sherlock Holmes*, *Cracker* and more recently *Criminal Minds* and *Mindhunter*. Unfortunately, as is so often the case, the reality is far removed from the images portrayed in the media – the truth is significantly less amazing and most profiles don't lead to successful identification and capture. In the famous Coals to Newcastle study (Copson, 1995), the success of profiling was seriously questioned as profiles led to an arrest in just 5 of the 184 cases studied.

Question time

How does the media portray offender profiling? Does it appear to be successful? What do the statistics above suggest about the success of offender profiling? Why do you think there is such a difference between the two?

New research

Thomas MacMillan (20 October 2017). Can criminal profilers really get inside the head of a killer?

The popularity of the Netflix series *Mindhunter* has renewed (if it ever went away) the public interest in the use of offender profiling and the question of whether it's possible to use interviews with serial killers to establish profiles of future killers and the usefulness of offender profiling in general. In this article, MacMillan looks at some of the research into profiling to see whether the claims made by TV shows have any basis in the real use of offender profiling.

MacMillan explains how modern profiling began with the use of the techniques by James Brussel and his profile of the Mad Bomber of New York City and the fact that when caught, he was single and wearing a buttoned double-breasted suit – two of the things that had been predicted by Brussel. Despite the fact that most of Brussel's other predictions were completely incorrect, the mystique of profiling was born.

The article goes on to question how profiling has been used in other cases, particularly the hunt for a sniper who was terrorising the Washington DC area in the early 2000s, when profilers had suggested that the sniper would be a white man in his 20s to 30s driving a white van. The actual snipers were two black men, one aged 17 and the other 40, who were using a blue sedan car, who had actually been stopped by police two hours before one of their attacks but weren't questioned, as they didn't fit the profile.

The article uses material from criminologist Dan Kennedy who argues that in spite of the lack of success, profiling is still regarded as popular by detectives who have used the technique, although Kennedy argues that it may be because the detectives want to justify the time and money spent on the profiles. One former FBI profiler, Mark Safarik, suggested that unlike the media presentation, good profilers are actually quite cautious, avoid overstepping the mark and are mainly involved in just narrowing down suspects, rather than trying to identify a specific individual. However, the interest in profiling in films and TV shows no sign of relenting and, according to Kennedy, there is a simple reason and that is, 'It hangs around in the public mind because it's cool'.

Question time

What does this research tell us about the usefulness of offender profiling?

Should we believe what we see on TV programmes like *Mindhunter*?

What is profiling mostly used for?

Explanations for crime

The attempt to determine the causes of crime has been going on for hundreds of years and the causes have ranged from the sublime to the ridiculous. The explanations are generally divided between the biological causes, which might suggest that criminals are simply born that way, and the psychological causes, which focus more on the idea that criminality has developed due to a range of factors occurring during the life of an individual.

Biological explanations focus on historical factors such as the atavistic form (physical characteristics, particular facial), genetic and neural (brain structure) explanations, whereas psychological explanations focus on a range of factors including personality, cognitive processes, differential association (the type of people you associate with) as well as psychodynamic explanations.

Activity 2

Consider the factors mentioned above as part of the biological and psychological explanations and try to explain what each of them might say about the causes of crime in the table below:

Factors related to the cause of crime	Possible explanations
Atavistic form (facial features)	
Genetics	
Brain structure	
The criminal personality	
Cognitive processes	
Differential association	
Psychodynamic explanations	

Question time

Which of these factors do you think provides the best explanation?
Is it possible to accept just one or would it be beneficial to take an interactionist approach?

Dealing with offending behaviour

One of the most difficult areas of forensic psychology is concerned with what do we do with offenders once we have caught them and how can we try to make sure that they don't offend again. This has been in the past, and continues to be today, something that provides a great deal of discussion for everyone from taxi drivers to journalists and is something that most people have an opinion about. The argument usually comes down to a question of whether we should punish offenders more severely or try to do what we can to make them better people, retribution vs rehabilitation.

Consequently, the ways of dealing with offending behaviour cover the use of custodial sentencing for criminals, including the problem of recidivism (re-offending), behaviour modification while in custody (token economy) and the use of anger management and restorative justice programmes.

New research

Esther van Ginneken (2016). The pain and purpose of punishment: A subjective perspective. Howard League – What is Justice? Working Papers 22/2016.

In research for The Howard League for Penal Reform (an organisation associated with changing the way we punish criminals), van Ginneken argues that although the aims of sentencing criminals to imprisonment may be punishment and the reduction of crime, the actual effect may be the opposite.

She argues that the current sentencing framework is working on the basis of a flawed understanding of the experience of prison sentences from the point of view of those at the sharp end, the criminals themselves. She suggests that the experience of imprisonment varies depending on individual circumstances and that some criminals will find the use of alternative punishments such as probation orders and community service more difficult than spending time in prison.

The current system, she argues, fails to communicate to prisoners what they are trying to achieve and as such the experience of prison can be seen to be less severe than expected, leading to a feeling that they got off easily. Consequently, imprisonment achieves neither rehabilitation nor deterrence and the problem of recidivism continues. The argument put forward is for a system that not only communicates more clearly the intention of the punishment a criminal is receiving but also involves them as active participants in shaping their own punishment. In practical terms, this would mean having a discussion, with input from the offender, the victim and the probation service, about the best sentence to impose on a prisoner so that we not only get the fairest result but also the most effective for the individual and for society.

Question time

What does this article tell us about the use of imprisonment for dealing with offenders?

What do you think of the suggestion to involve the criminal in a discussion about the best sentence?

Is it a case of 'if it was easy to fix then someone would have already done it by now'?

Summary

This introduction should have got you ready for more of this kind of discussion and will hopefully aid you in your further understanding of these fascinating topics.

Chapter 2
Offender profiling

Spec check

Offender profiling: the top-down approach, including organised and disorganised types of offender; the bottom-up approach, including investigative psychology and geographical profiling.

AO1 (Knowledge and understanding): Offender profiling

What is offender profiling?

In the introduction to this volume, I looked at the comparison between the public perception of offender profiling (as shown in the media) and the reality (as practiced by real-life profilers). The media would have us believe that the profiler has some, almost, supernatural ability to identify and get inside the head of the criminal. However, in reality profiling takes a lot of hard work and is usually gained from the use of more traditional methods of psychological research. The profiler will use observations of the crime scene, analysis of data reported by the police about the specific circumstances of the crime, e.g. time of day as well as evidence from interviews with witnesses and other relevant parties. All of this may (or may not) help the profiler come up with information about the likely characteristics of the offender, e.g. age, occupation and location.

The aims of profiling do, in general terms, fit the media creation, which is to identify unknown criminals when traditional police methods have not done so. More specifically, the profiler will be brought in when the police have little to go on and need to find some way of narrowing down the potential list of suspects in order that traditional police methods can be more focused on certain areas or types of people.

There are two general approaches to profiling: the top-down approach has traditionally been associated with the US and has been used in the past by the FBI; the bottom-up approach has traditionally been associated with the UK and has been used by British profilers such as David Canter.

The top-down approach

This approach developed from the work of the FBI behavioural science unit and in particular the work of John E. Douglas and Robert K. Ressler who were used as inspiration for the characters Holden Ford and Bill Tench in the fictional TV series *Mindhunter*. Just like the TV series, during the 1970s Douglas and Ressler interviewed 36 notorious serial killers in order to develop a method of identifying unknown killers from these interviews, with the information gained being used as a template for future killers and rapists.

This approach takes the information gained from the accounts given by the offenders and from this creates a typological approach within which there are two types, **organised offenders** and **disorganised offenders**. These two types of offenders are associated with certain forms of behaviour that can then be analysed in relation to the specific features of the crime scene, which will then hopefully lead to further specific characteristics of an offender who may typically adopt such forms of behaviour and from that it should be possible to narrow down the suspects (see Table 2.1). This typology should allow the police and FBI to create a profile of an offender that would provide a smaller pool of suspects so that the investigation could now become more targeted.

Table 2.1 Organised and disorganised types

Type of offender	Features of the crime/scene	Offender characteristics
Organised	Planned High level of control Weapon present Body hidden or moved from crime scene Evidence cleared from scene Aggression before death	Above average IQ Skilled occupation Socially competent Sexually competent Mobile, so may live far away Living with partner High birth order, e.g. eldest Inconsistent discipline as a child Little change in behaviour after crime Follows crime reports in the media
Disorganised	Spontaneous Uncontrolled Weapon absent Body not hidden or left at crime scene Evidence left uncleared Sex after death	Average or below average IQ Unskilled occupation Socially incompetent Sexually incompetent Lives near crime scene Living alone Low birth order, e.g. youngest Harsh discipline as a child Major behaviour change after crime Does not follow crime in the media

The criminal profile generating process

Douglas et al. (1986) describe the process of generating a profile as a five-stage process, with the sixth being the apprehension of the offender:

1. Profiling inputs stage – all the case materials relevant to the crime are studied, e.g. autopsy reports, background information on the victim, as well as forensic evidence from the scene, such as photographs.
2. Decision process models stage – involves arranging all the inputs into meaningful patterns concerning the type of murder, whether the murder was premeditated or not and other factors related to time, location and the level of risk associated with both victim and offender.
3. Crime assessment stage – involves classifying the crime as either organised or disorganised (see Table 2.1).
4. Criminal profile stage – involves creating hypotheses relating to the likely characteristics of the offender (see Table 2.1).
5. Investigation stage – the profile is used and if necessary reviewed in the light of new evidence.

Question time

What are the main differences between organised and disorganised offenders? Are there likely to be other types of offenders? Is it possible to have a mixed approach?

The bottom-up approach

This approach is most famously associated with the British profiler David Canter and the focus of this approach is not on the data gained from the accounts of previous offenders (like the top-down approach) but is focused on the data gained from the crime scene itself. This systematic analysis of the crime scene allows the profiler to take a more thoroughly objective approach as they scrutinise in detail the behavioural evidence of the crime itself without the restrictions that might arise from having preconceived ideas developed from interviews with other, similar offenders.

Investigative psychology

The best known example of the bottom-up approach is the practice of **investigative psychology** developed by David Canter (1990), which involves using a statistical approach to break the crime scene down into the behavioural characteristics identified at the crime scene. These can then, alongside psychological theory, be used to establish patterns of behaviour that can be applied to this (and other) crime scenes to create a likely profile of the offender. Using this approach, Canter was able to develop five factors that can be applied to the crime scene and identify important characteristics related to the identity of the offender (see Table 2.2).

Table 2.2 The five factors used in investigative psychology and their description

Factor	Description of factor
Interpersonal coherence	The behaviour shown at the crime scene will be similar to that shown in everyday life.
Time and space	Information about when and where the crime is committed might provide clues as to where the offender lives and works.
Forensic awareness	The extent to which they show an understanding of the need to hide forensic evidence will indicate their criminal history.
Criminal career	The behaviour shown at the crime scene is likely to have been shown at other crimes committed by this offender and this can provide clues to their behaviour in future crimes.
Criminal characteristics	The characteristics identified can then be compared to similar crimes to categorise the offender and aid police investigations.

Think!

Does this bottom-up approach seem to be better or worse than the top-down approach?

What are the main advantages and disadvantages?

Geographical profiling

This is another bottom-up approach, which pretty much does exactly what it says, i.e. uses information taken from the geographical details of the crime to identify the likely location of the offender's home or base. Geographical profiling, also known as crime mapping, was first put forward by Kim Rossmo (2000) and involves examining the geographical connections between the locations of a series of crimes to try to understand where an offender is based and where they are likely to strike again. This involves the use of a computer system called Rigel, which combines the information gained about the spatial relationship of the offender's crimes with environmental crime theory and mathematics to create a 2D map that can be laid over a street map to identify the likely home location of an offender.

This approach was also used by David Canter (1994) in his circle theory, which suggests that the location of an offender's crimes are likely to form a circle around their home location. From this Canter identified a model of offender behaviour called 'the marauder' who was someone who would travel from their base at the centre of this circle to various locations relatively close to their home to commit crimes. However, Canter also identified another model called 'the commuter' who was someone who would travel away from their base to commit crimes and as such would be much more difficult to locate. However, these could be identified as marauder crimes as they tended to be closer together than commuter crimes and would still be likely to occur in a place that was known to the offender.

Mini Plenary

Without referring back to the text, provide definitions of the following terms:

Top-down approach _____

Organised and disorganised offenders _____

Bottom-up approach _____

Investigative psychology _____

Geographical profiling _____

AO2 (Application of knowledge): How does this apply in practice?

The case of the Green River Killer

In July 1982, a 16-year-old girl went missing in Washington State USA and her dead body was later found in the Green River. This was believed to be the first in a series of murders carried out by Gary Ridgway who later became known as the Green River killer, as so many of his victims were dumped in or near there. Ridgway was particularly active in the two years after this date but the police investigating the case had not been able to find hard evidence to catch the killer.

In an unusual twist, involving a similar situation to that depicted in the film *The Silence of the Lambs*, the detective involved in the case, Robert Keppel, was contacted by serial killer **Ted Bundy**. Bundy offered to provide some insights as to the identity of the killer and Keppel decided, as they had been struggling with case, to accept the offer and interview Bundy.

Although the information provided by Bundy didn't directly help in the apprehension of Ridgway, it did provide some useful insights into the mind of a serial killer, e.g. Bundy was able to suggest that the killer would revisit the site of his crimes, as that was something Bundy himself had done. However, the information was unhelpful at the time, as the media were also patrolling the area with a helicopter, which served to provide an easy means of seeing the stake-out cars used by the police. However, it was later found that Ridgway had revisited the crime scene to have sex with the dead bodies and this did provide some DNA evidence, which was used in his conviction.

Question time

How does this case relate to the top-down approach?

Does this case suggest that interviewing previous offenders is useful?

Why did Bundy offer to help in this case?

The case of the railway rapist

In the 1980s, David Canter was called on to assist the police in their investigation into a series of rapes that had occurred since around 1982. At least 19 women had been raped near to railway stations, which is how the offender obtained the nickname of the railway rapist. The crimes were getting worse, progressing to murder around 1985 to 1986 and the police had called on the services of Canter, as they had few clues to the identity of the rapist/murderer.

Canter provided a profile that was so accurate that it helped the police to focus more seriously on someone who had already come to their attention in the process of conducting **operation hart** – that man was John Duffy (see Table 2.3).

The profile was very accurate and, as a consequence, Duffy was arrested. However, there was no similar profile of his accomplice (David Mulcahy) who wasn't convicted of his part in the crimes till 2000.

Table 2.3 The profile of the characteristics of the railway rapist and the characteristics of John Duffy

Canter's profile	John Duffy
Knowledge of the railway	Had worked on the railway as a carpenter
Lived in Kilburn/Cricklewood	Lived in Kilburn
Mid to late twenties	Aged 29
Physically small	Five foot four inches tall
A loner with few friends	Only two friends (one was his accomplice)
Poor relationship with women but married	Violent to wife and separated
Knowledge of police procedures	Arrested in the past

How does the case of John Duffy fit with the five factors used in the process of investigative psychology?

Does it also relate to geographical profiling?

The case of Rachel Nickel

Both of the cases described above are relevant to the success of profiling but there have been cases where profiling hasn't been so successful. One such case is the murder of Rachel Nickell.

In 1992, Rachel Nickell was sexually assaulted and brutally stabbed in front of her two-year-old son on Wimbledon Common. Her body was later found by a dog walker with her son next to her desperately trying to get her to wake up. As her son was the only witness and they had interviewed many suspects and arrested and released 32 other men, the police called on the help of a profiler, Paul Britton, who had become well-known for his profiling work.

Working together, Britton and the police came up with a potential suspect in the form of Colin Stagg, who was local and had been known to walk his dog on the common (he had been on the common on the morning of the murder). Crucially he fitted the photofit that had been in the press (leading to a number of people identifying Stagg) and the profile created by Britton of a loner with an obsession with knives and sadistic sexual fantasies. However, there was still no real evidence against him and so the police used an attractive female detective in a 'honey trap' in an attempt to get him to admit to the crime. Stagg was contacted by the detective over a period of months with suggestions that she might be interested in a sexual relationship until finally the police decided they had enough against him to take it to court. However, the judge felt they had very little and the case was thrown out with the police claiming they had no other suspects!

The actual killer of Rachel Nickell was a serial rapist named Robert Napper, who was eventually convicted of her murder in 2008, following the discovery of forensic evidence linking him to the offence. However, the case dealt a massive blow to the credibility of profiling in the UK and forced the police to review their use of it in such cases.

Question time

What do all these cases tell us about the success of offender profiling?

Does the case of Rachel Nickell suggest that the police should stop using profiling?

What other factors caused the police to identify Stagg as the potential killer?

In the past, the assumption has been that offender profiling is only applicable to crimes such as serial murder or sex crimes. However, in recent years it has started to be used for a range of other crimes, such as arson, burglary and even terror offences.

With reference to the top-down and bottom-up approach to profiling, explain why profiling may have only been seen to be useful for certain crimes in the past but is now seen to be relevant to a wider range of crimes?

AO3 (Analysis and evaluation of knowledge): How useful is offender profiling?

Can profilers outperform non-profilers in terms of accuracy?

In 1976, the former editor of *Psychology Today*, Colin Campbell, posed the question of whether profilers were any better at predicting behaviour than a bartender, which opens up the question of whether profilers are simply using speculation and intuition in their attempts to identify offenders. This is a criticism that has been particularly aimed at the top-down approach, as it has relied so much on the insights gained from previous offenders, which is then used by profilers to inform their decisions about who may have committed a crime.

In order to assess this kind of claim, Brent Snook (2007) and his colleagues conducted research on behalf of the American Association for Correctional and Forensic Psychology in the form of a **narrative review** and **meta-analysis** of a large number of articles and studies to see what procedures were being used and whether profilers were any better than non-profilers.

Overall, they found the articles published were frequently working on the basis of **anecdotal evidence** and intuition rather than scientific evidence and facts. From the meta-analysis, they came to the conclusion that profilers were only slightly better than non-profilers in identifying important characteristics about an unknown offender and that overall, profiling appeared to be an extraneous and redundant technique for use in criminal investigations and would remain so until profiling began to use more scientific procedures.

Can profiling be used for more than just rape and murder?

One of the criticisms, if you can all it a criticism, aimed at profiling is that it can *only* be used for cases of very serious crimes, such as rape or murder and that it isn't much use for less serious crimes, such as property crime or arson. This criticism has been particularly aimed at the use of the top-down approach as it is so closely aligned with the use of interviews with serial killers and rapists and as such the information gained is only applicable to those crimes.

However, in relation to the use of geographical profiling at least, there has been some successful use in a case of serial arson. The police force in Irvine, California, had been struggling to catch an offender believed to be responsible for a series of arsons until the force's Crime Analysis Unit used Rigel to come up with a geographic profile of the case and subsequently came up with a highly populated residential area as the likely home base of the suspect, which, initially at least, failed to reveal the identity of the offender. However, they were able to use the information to identify the next likely location that the arsonist would attack and undercover officers were able to patrol the area and catch the female offender in the act.

This suggests that while geographical profiling may not be able to directly solve cases, it can be used as another tool for narrowing down the location of offenders and combined with the normal police analytical skills and working with crime maps, it can be successful in all forms of serial crime.

How should the success of profiling be judged?

A regular issue in the study of offender profiling is the question of whether the profile provided is accurate, which can be seen both from cases where it was incredibly successful like that of Canter's profile of John Duffy and Britton's unsuccessful profile of Colin Stagg. Further analysis of this success comes from Copson's (1995) coals to Newcastle study in which he found that profiling has only led to an arrest in five of the 184 cases studied. However, it may be that judging the success of profiling in this purely quantitative way may not be the most appropriate approach and asking the consumers of the service, the police investigators involved in the case, may be better.

Gekoski and Gray (2011) argued for this approach and sought to find out whether the police satisfaction previously identified by studies (Trager and Brewster, 2001; and Snook et al., 2007) was real or a result of the quantitative survey method used to gain this result. Consequently, Gekoski and Gray employed a more qualitative approach with a sample of 11 officers who had previously worked with a profiler on 34 cases, an average of three times each.

They found that, on the whole, the officers were dissatisfied with the usefulness of the profiler, even if what they were saying was accurate. There were many reasons given for this dissatisfaction, among the most common were that: the leads were too general; the advice was like common sense (my mum could have told me that); they were things they already knew (selling coals to Newcastle); and even went against PACE guidelines, so could have jeopardised the whole case. There were some positives though as the officers also said that: it was useful to have a fresh pair of eyes; the profile provided some backup; and everything else had been tried so it was worth a try.

The overall conclusion of the study was that officers were generally dissatisfied with the use of profiling and that, in spite of any gains, the use of profiling was mostly a waste of time and money. However, this was quite a small sample and it is difficult to draw conclusions from this, particularly when it was taken in a way that may itself create problems of demand characteristics and bias.

Top-down or bottom-up, which is best?

The top-down approach is one that takes a more nomothetic approach to the study of offenders and creates a typology that could be potentially applied to a number of people of a given type based on theoretical principles derived from people of a similar type. There are a number of positives and negatives to this approach: on the one hand it can provide insights that can be used as a guide to the sort of person likely to commit such an act, which could guide the police towards a smaller group of people that fit the type; on the other hand, the information is so general that it could be applied to so many people as to be completely unhelpful.

The bottom-up approach is one that takes a more idiographic approach as it attempts to draw conclusions from the specifics of the particular crime scene and has the potential therefore to produce more of a tailored profile that would be applicable to fewer individuals, which could therefore narrow down the field of investigation more tightly, making the job of the police a lot easier. However, as we have seen, this process can be somewhat hit and miss and may provide a very accurate profile that leads the police straight to the correct individual in the case of John Duffy, or lead the police straight to the incorrect individual in the case of Colin Stagg.

Furthermore, although the bottom-up approach may appear to be more idiographic and therefore not based on the creation of certain types, it still led Canter to the creation of the marauder and commuter types in his use of geographical profiling. Consequently, it is difficult to say whether one is all that different from the other, never mind whether one is better than the other.

Mini plenary

Using the evaluation points above, try to evaluate the following statement:

Offender profiling is a waste of police time and resources.

Arguments for	Arguments against

A modern issue: How has profiling changed and is it more or less useful today?

In modern times, there have been advances in all areas of police work but particularly in the use of DNA evidence. However, this still leaves open the question of how we find someone in order to test and compare their DNA in the first place. Consequently, it may be that profiling is still necessary but we also want to know whether it can still be successful and if it has improved from the past.

New research

Bryanna Fox and David P. Farrington, What have we learned from offender profiling? A systematic review and meta-analysis of 40 years of research. Psychological Bulletin, 2018.

In the article, Fox and Farrington set out to consider the success or otherwise of offender profiling after 40 years of its use and research into its success, to establish whether it has been successful and how much progress has been made in those 40 years.

In order to do this, Fox and Farrington conducted a systematic review and meta-analysis of 426 publications looking at the use of offender profiling dating from 1976 to 2016. They were particularly interested in doing this since the most extensive research into offender profiling (Snook at al., 2008) was published a decade ago and it might be necessary to take stock of where we are now.

The researchers found that in contrast to the past, virtually none of the current research was being done by the FBI and most was being done by academics in Britain and Canada and there have been major improvements in the scientific rigour and self-assessment being conducted in this field. The analysis of the ability of profiles to provide a link between the case and individual offenders was that the area is statistically sophisticated, the accuracy of the profiles was strong to moderate and that if the work continues in this way then profiling could be very successful and help to make the world a safer place.

Finally, Fox and Farrington return to the question posed by Campbell in 1976 as to whether profilers are better at this than a bartender and concede that the answer still remains unknown, despite the fact that profiling has come a long way since then. However, they go on to suggest that if the use of advanced scientific and statistical procedures continue, then it is highly likely that the answer will be yes.

Question time

What does this article tell us about the use of offender profiling?
Does this suggest that profiling is more successful now than in the past?
What is the way forward for profiling?

Chapter plenary

1. What is offender profiling?
2. What is the top-down approach?
3. What is the bottom-up approach?
4. What is involved in investigative psychology?
5. What is geographical profiling?

6. What does the case of the green river killer tell us about the use of profiling?

7. What do the cases of the railway rapist and the Rachel Nickell murder tell us about the success of profiling?

8. Can profilers outperform non-profilers in terms of accuracy?

9. Can profiling be used for more than just rape or murder?

10. How should the success of profiling be judged?

11. Top-down or bottom-up, which is best?

12. What have we learned from profiling in 40 years?

Glossary

Key word	Definition
Anecdotal evidence	Evidence that has no scientific basis and is just based on ideas developed from previous experiences.
Bottom-up approach	An approach to profiling based on the scientific analysis of the crime scene to provide behavioural clues as to the identification of the current offender.
Circle theory	An approach used by David Canter that tries to use the spatial distribution of the crimes to draw a circle around the likely location of the offender's home or workplace.
Disorganised offender	A type of offender that shows little planning and the victim is not targeted. They also show little concern about 'cleaning' the crime scene.
Geographical profiling	An approach to profiling based on the work of Kim Rossmo that focuses on the location of a series of crimes to identify the likely home location of the offender.
Honey trap	A kind of police operation that involves a female undercover police officer trying to trap a suspect into revealing their crime due to their sexual desire for the undercover officer.
Investigative psychology	An approach to profiling based on the work of David Canter that uses a statistical approach to break the crime scene down into behavioural characteristics.
Meta-analysis	A method of research using data from a number of previous studies to try to establish an overall trend.
Narrative review	A comprehensive and critical analysis of the current knowledge of a topic.
Organised offender	A type of offender that plans their offence and targets their victim. They like to 'clean' the crime scene.

Key word	Definition
PACE (Police and Criminal Conduct Evidence Act, 1984)	A code of conduct that should be followed by police officers when investigating a crime, particularly in relation to their dealings with potential suspects.
The commuter	A type of criminal identified by Canter who offends in a circle that is some distance away from their own home.
The marauder	A type of criminal identified by Canter who offends within the confines of the circle around their home location.
Top-down approach	An approach to profiling based on interviewing previous offenders to provide information that may be useful in the identification of future offenders.

Plenary: Exam-style questions and answers with advisory comments

Question 1.

Outline what is meant by the top-down approach and the bottom-up approach in relation to offender profiling. [4 marks]

Marks for this question: AO1 = 4

Advice: In a question like this, it's important to make sure you are outlining the definition of each of these two terms in the context of offender profiling. The question does not ask you to explain the difference between them so each can be focused on separately. There is no need to provide any analysis or evaluation as all of the marks are for AO1: Knowledge and understanding.

Possible answer: The top-down approach is an approach to profiling based on the interviewing of previous offenders to provide information that may be useful in the identification of future offenders. It is associated with the FBI who interviewed 36 serial killers to help them understand the motives of such offenders.

The bottom-up approach is an approach to profiling based on the scientific analysis of the crime scene to provide behavioural clues as to the identification of the current offender. It is associated with the work of David Canter who used a statistical approach to break the crime scene down into the behavioural characteristics identified at the crime scene.

Question 2.

Discuss the top-down approach and/or the bottom-up approach to offender profiling. [16 marks]

Marks for this question: AO1 = 6 and AO3 = 10

Advice: This question asks about two different approaches using the command of and/or, which means that you need to make a decision about whether to just focus on one in lots of detail or both in less detail. There will need to be a breadth/depth trade-off as just doing one will require more depth and doing two will require greater breadth. This question is looking for both skills of knowledge and understanding and analysis and evaluation. As there are 6 marks for AO1 and 10 for AO3, there should be greater emphasis on the evaluation. However, all such extended writing questions are marked holistically and therefore it is important that the knowledge is accurate and detailed and that the evaluation is clear and effective.

Possible answer: The top-down approach is an approach to profiling based on the interviewing of previous offenders to provide information that may be useful in the identification of future offenders. It is associated with the FBI who interviewed 36 serial killers to help them understand the motives of such offenders. This approach takes the information gained from the accounts given by the offenders and from this creates a typological approach within which there are two types, organised offenders and disorganised offenders. These two types of offender are associated with certain forms of behaviour that can then be analysed in relation to the specific features of the crime scene, which will then hopefully lead to further specific characteristics of an offender who may typically adopt such forms of behaviour and from that it should be possible to narrow down the suspects.

The bottom-up approach is an approach to profiling based on the scientific analysis of the crime scene to provide behavioural clues as to the identification of the current offender. It is associated with the work of David Canter who used a statistical approach to break the crime scene down into the behavioural characteristics identified at the crime scene. Using this approach, Canter was able to develop five factors that can be applied to the crime scene and identify important characteristics related to the identity of the offender, e.g. interpersonal coherence, whereby the behaviour shown at the crime scene will be similar to that shown in everyday life. The other four factors were: time and space – information about when and where the crime was committed might give clues to where they live/work; forensic awareness – do they show an awareness of the need to hide forensic evidence; criminal career – the behaviour shown at other crimes might give clues about their future behaviour; and criminal characteristics – being able to categorise the offender as one type or another.

Both of these approaches have been used successfully at times, with the top-down approach being used in the case of the green river killer, who was eventually apprehended with some help from the serial killer Ted Bundy. Bundy gave some important information about the killer's desire to return the scene of his murders, which eventually led to the finding of DNA evidence from one of these scenes and the conviction of Gary Ridgway.

Similarly, the bottom-up approach was used in the successful capture of the railway rapist, John Duffy from a profile provided by David Canter. Canter was able to figure out that Duffy was a former railway employee, that he lived near the area where most of the attacks took place, but also that he was short, was single or divorced and even his age.

However, profiling isn't always this successful, as can be seen from the use of profiling in the case of Colin Stagg, the man originally accused of killing Rachel Nickell, in which case the profile was completely wrong. Further analysis of this success comes from Copson's coals to Newcastle study in which he found that profiling has only led to an arrest in five of the 184 cases studied.

Furthermore, Gekoski and Gray found that the police officers that have used the services of a profiler were dissatisfied with their usefulness, even if what they were saying was actually accurate. There were many reasons given for this dissatisfaction, among the most common were that: the leads were too general; the advice was like common sense (my mum could have told me that); they were things they already knew (selling coals to Newcastle); and even went against **PACE** guidelines, so could have jeopardised the whole case. There were some positives though, as the officers also said: it was useful to have a fresh pair of eyes; the profile provided some backup; and everything else had been tried so it was worth a try.

The judgement about which approach is better could be analysed in terms of nomothetic vs idiographic approaches. The top-down approach attempts to create general types from its analysis and as such could be described as nomothetic. There are a number of positives and negatives to this approach: on the one hand it can provide insights that can be used as a guide to the sort of person that is likely to commit such an act, which could guide the police towards a smaller group of people that fit the type; on the other hand, the information is so general that it could be applied to so many people as to be completely unhelpful.

Whereas the bottom-up approach works more idiographically by trying to identify the characteristics of the specific offender, in this case by a focus on the specific features of this crime scene. This has the potential therefore to produce a more tailored profile that would be applicable to fewer individuals, which could therefore narrow down the field of investigation more tightly, making the job of the police a lot easier. However, this process can be somewhat hit and miss and may provide a very accurate profile that leads the police straight to the correct individual, in the case of John Duffy, or leads the police straight to the incorrect individual, in the case of Colin Stagg.

However, in a review of the success of profiling over the last 40 years, Fox and Farrington found that profiling was increasingly becoming more statistical and scientific and that if it continued in that way, it was likely to be more successful, which fits with the bottom-up approach. It has also been found that in recent times, the FBI has changed its focus to be much more in line with Canter's approach and the use of investigative psychology, which suggests that it is the bottom-up approach that stood the test of time.

References

Canter, D. and Heritage, R. (1990). A multivariate model of sexual offence behaviour: Developments in 'offender profiling'. *The Journal of Forensic Psychiatry*, 1(2): 185–212.

Canter, D.V. and Gregory, A. (1994). Identifying the residential location of rapists. *Journal of the Forensic Science Society*, 34(3): 169–175.

Douglas, J.E., Ressler, R.K., Burgess, A.W. and Harman, C.R. (1986). Criminal profiling from crime scene analysis. *Behavioural Sciences & the Law*, 4(4): 401–421.

Fox, B. and Farrington, D.P. (2018) What have we learned from offender profiling? A systematic review and meta-analysis of 40 years of research. *Psychological Bulletin*, 144(12): 1247.

Gekoski, A. and Gray, J.M. (2011). 'It may be true, but how's it helping?': Police detectives' views of the operational usefulness of offender profiling. *International Journal of Police Science & Management*, 13(2): 103–116.

Rossmo, D.K. (2000). *Geographic Profiling. Boca Raton*, FL: CRC Press.

Snook, B., Eastwood, J., Gendreau, P., Goggin, C. and Cullen, R.M. (2007) Taking stock of criminal profiling: A narrative review and meta-analysis. *Criminal Justice and Behavior*, 34(4): 437–453.

Trager, J. and Brewster, J. (2001). The effectiveness of psychological profiles. *Journal of Police and Criminal Psychology*, 16(1): 20–28.

Chapter 3
Biological explanations of offending behaviour

Spec check

Biological explanations of offending behaviour: an historical approach (atavistic form); genetics and neural explanations.

AO1 (Knowledge and understanding): Biological explanations of offending behaviour

An historical approach to offending

Although the widespread use of offender profiling is relatively new, there have been experts helping the police to identify offenders for much longer, most famously in the case of Jack the Ripper. Most of these experts were academics who were able to apply scientific principles to the process in order to provide some basic ideas about the characteristics of offenders. One such academic was Professor Cesare Lombroso who became known as the father of criminology for his attempt to explain the basis of offending behaviour in his book *L'Huomo Delinquente* (Criminal Man) first published in 1876 in Italy and then translated into English in 1911.

In the book, Lombroso sets out what was to become one of the most influential attempts to explain the causes of offending behaviour and gave Lombroso the status of one of the leading experts in the understanding of criminal behaviour at the time. He discovered that criminal behaviour is **innate** and therefore criminals are destined to behave in that way because of the personality characteristics that are associated with their evolution (or lack of it). Lombroso says that he stumbled upon his great discovery while examining the dead body of Giuseppe Villella, a thief and arsonist. Lombroso noticed that the shape of the skull resembled that of an ape, specifically related to an indentation at the base of Villella's skull, which led him to the idea that the criminal was a throwback to some primitive form that was genetically different to modern humans, the **atavistic form**.

What is the atavistic form?

This great discovery developed into the idea that criminals were so different from modern (non-criminal) humans that they could be identified by the shape and structure of their face and head. Lombroso came up with certain physiological characteristics that could be used as a guide to understanding the precise criminal tendencies of individual criminals, in other words, it is possible to tell the crime that someone is likely to commit from looking at their face. In general terms, this meant that a criminal would have some combination of the following: a protruding jaw, a low sloping forehead, large ears, asymmetrical faces and insensitivity to pain, potentially alongside extra nipples, fingers or toes.

These initial findings led Lombroso to conduct further research into the physical characteristics of criminals by studying the facial features and skull measurements of nearly 4,000 living criminals and the skulls of 400 dead criminals. From this, Lombroso was able to come up with the idea that specific facial characteristics were associated with specific crimes (see Table 3.1).

Table 3.1 The facial characteristics associated with certain crimes (Lombroso, 1911)

Crime	Facial characteristics
Theft	Thick close eyebrows, squashed nose, thin hair, sloping foreheads.
Rape	Jug ears, sparkling eyes, swollen lips and eyelids.
Arson	Soft child-like skin, long feminine hair.
Murder	Bloodshot eyes, large hawk-like noses, thin lips and broad cheekbones.

Think!

Do these characteristics provide us with a useful guide to what a criminal is like? If not, why not?

Could you identify the crimes committed by these individuals from the characteristics given?

Genetic explanations

Although Lombroso's work was itself quite primitive (it lacked the scientific rigour of modern theories), it did set the scene for the idea that offending behaviour could be genetic and therefore passed down from one generation to the next. Furthermore, it did move the debate away from religious or spiritual explanations that put offending down to the work of the devil or of evil spirits.

The genetic argument has become increasingly prominent in most areas of psychology, partially due to the work of the **human genome project** who have been able to map out the entire human genome and have helped to move the debate forwards as to the possibility that all forms of human behaviour may have a natural basis rather than simply being learned from experience.

Twin studies

Another part of the impetus for the interest in genetic explanations of offending behaviour has come from studies of the only genetically identical individuals on the planet – MZ twins. If we can show that both sets of identical twins have the same tendencies towards criminal behaviour then we can go some way to showing that offending is in some way genetic. Most of the research in this area has compared genetically identical MZ twins with non-identical DZ twins in order to see if the concordance rates are different for each, which might indicate a genetic influence on crime. The early research in this area was criticised on the basis that it was heavily influenced by the mood of eugenics at the time, particularly those studies published around the time of the rise of the Nazis in Germany (Lange, 1929; Rosanoff, Handy and Rosanoff, 1934). One of the first twin studies to take a more objective approach to the study of crime was by Christiansen (1977) who used the Danish national twin registry to identify over 3,500 twin pairs who were then checked against police records, finding that the concordance rate for MZ twins was 33 per cent and for DZ twins was 12 per cent, suggesting a degree of heritability in crime. Stronger evidence comes from the review of 13 studies conducted by Raine (1993) showing a concordance rate for MZ twins of 52 per cent and for DZ twins of 21 per cent. However, it is widely believed that the similar treatment given to identical twins may account for some of this difference.

Adoption studies

In an attempt to break away from the problem of similar environments affecting the results of these studies, some psychologists have advocated the use of adoption studies which, it is believed, may offer the opportunity of comparing the individual with both their biological and adopted parents. This can show whether they are more similar to their biological parents (supporting a genetic influence) or more similar to their adopted parents (supporting an environmental influence).

One of the most famous studies of adoptees was conducted by Mednick et al. (1984) in which they studied over 6,000 male adoptees to identify their record of crime in comparison to both their biological and adoptive parents. They found that if the adoptive parents had a criminal record and the biological parents did not, then the son's conviction rate was 14.7 per cent but if the biological parents had a criminal record and the adoptive parents did not then the son's conviction rate was 20 per cent, suggesting a slight influence of genes over environment. However, this was only true for property crime and not for violent crime.

> **Think!**
>
> Do these studies show a difference between the influence of genes and environment on criminal behaviour? If so, is the difference significant?
>
> What other factors have not been considered in these studies?

Is there a criminal gene?

There have been many attempts to identify a gene for criminal behaviour, all of which have found it very difficult to identify a single gene that could be shown to be responsible for crime. However, some have identified genes that may be responsible for violent crime due to their link with aggression, so-called **candidate genes**.

One such gene is the **MAOA** gene, which is involved in the regulation of serotonin, dopamine and noradrenaline and it has been found that deficiencies in this gene are associated with aggression which could push some towards violent crime (Brunner et al., 1993). Other studies have found a more direct link between the gene and crime (Lea and Chambers, 2007 and Tiihonen et al., 2015) leading to the use of the term **warrior gene** to describe those with this abnormality, although this term does seem to glamourise the violent tendencies of these individuals, which seems rather inappropriate for violent criminals.

However, none of these studies have as yet been able to suggest that the gene is solely responsible for criminal behaviour, nor have they been able to isolate the effect of this gene from environmental influences. Consequently, it seems more reasonable to suggest that crime may be **polygenic** (Tielbeek et al., 2017) or that genes may interact with environmental factors to produce an increased tendency towards criminal activity (Caspi et al., 2002).

Question time

What does this tell us about whether crime is genetic or not?

In what ways would it be useful for us to find out? What problems would arise if we did find that crime is genetic?

What do you think it means to say that genes may interact with environmental factors to produce an increased tendency towards criminal activity? Have you come across this idea before?

Neural explanations

Neural explanations are focused on the structure and activity of the brain to identify if there are differences in these areas between criminals and non-criminals, which might help to explain the differences in behaviour between the two groups.

As we have already seen, there have been suggestions that genes regulating **serotonin**, **dopamine** and **noradrenaline** are involved in aggression and violence (Brunner et al., 1993) so it would seem reasonable to suggest that these neurotransmitters are involved in the production of aggression and therefore could be related to violent crime. Serotonin has been linked to the control of impulsive behaviour, therefore lower levels might bring on impulsive, violent reactions. Similarly, noradrenaline has been linked to the fight or flight response and abnormal levels could bring on violent reactions to perceived threats. The role of dopamine in aggression is less well understood but is involved in risk-taking and pleasure-seeking behaviour, which may explain **instrumental aggression**.

One of the most famous studies of the effect of brain structure and activity on violent crime was that of Raine et al. (1997) who studied the brains of 41 individuals charged with murder or manslaughter who had pleaded not guilty by reason of insanity to their crimes. Raine et al. used PET scans and were able to show that there was reduced activity in the prefrontal cortex (PFC) compared to a matched control group of 41 non-criminals. They also found activity differences in the amygdala, parietal cortex and corpus callosum, suggesting there may be a number of differences in brain activity that contribute to violent crime. In a later study (Raine et al., 2000), they found an 11 per cent reduction in the volume of grey matter in the PFC of subjects with antisocial personality disorder, suggesting that this part of the brain, which is particularly involved in the control of impulsive behaviour, may help to explain the behaviour of violent criminals.

Think!

What does the Raine study tell us about the causes of crime?

Do you think it makes a person less responsible for their crime?

Mini plenary

Using the information above, write a summary of biological explanations. It should answer the following questions?

What is meant by the atavistic form? How do twin studies and adoption studies research the idea that crime is genetic? Is there a criminal gene? What are the neural explanations of crime?

AO2 (Application of knowledge): How does this apply in practice?

Interleave me now

The genetic basis of behaviour

In the biological approach, the study of behavioural genetics considers the extent to which your genes influence your behaviour as well as your physical characteristics. On the one hand, Darwin was looking at the development of physical characteristics that increase your chance of survival and, as a result, increase the possibility that you will reproduce and pass on your genes. On the other hand, Darwin was also looking at the same process with behaviour, because if your behaviour increases your chance of survival then it is more likely to be passed down.

Genotype and phenotype

Genotype is the actual genetic make-up of an individual, whereas the phenotype is the way those genes are expressed through physical, behavioural and psychological characteristics. The phenotype is influenced by environmental factors such as lifestyle and possibly even exposure to significant events.

Table 3.2 Jim Fallon – do your genes make you a murderer?

The research quoted above has shown that genes may be linked to criminal behaviour and in particular aggression. The MAOA gene could be responsible for causing some people to become violent, aggressive and possibly even murderous.

Jim Fallon, professor of psychiatry at the University of California, was looking into this phenomenon when he discovered that he himself had a family history that involved an awful lot of murderers. So, he got tested and found that he himself had a gene combination associated with violent psychopathic behaviour.

As he puts it: 'People with far less dangerous genetics become killers and are psychopaths than what I have. I have almost all of them'.

However, far from being a murderer, Jim is a respected professor.

His explanation is that his happy childhood helped to protect him from this potential violent legacy. He believes that having the gene combined with childhood events that are abusive or in some way deeply traumatic could take you in that direction. However, without those events, it is a lot less likely to happen.

Mini plenary

Jim has recently found out that many of his ancestors are criminal and a number of them actual murderers. Jim hasn't got any criminal tendencies but he's worried that he might inherit some of his ancestors' 'criminal genes' and do something bad himself, even though he's had such a good upbringing and happy childhood.

Use the idea of genotype and phenotype to explain why Jim shouldn't have anything to worry about.

_____

_____

_____

_____

_____

_____

_____

_____

AO3 (Analysis and evaluation of knowledge): How useful is this explanation for crime?

Why is there a problem with causation in biological explanations?

A lot of the evidence for the biological causes of crime comes from studies that intend to show an association between crime and some other variable, be it facial characteristics, genes or brain structure and brain activity. Twin studies have been able to show concordance rates of around 50 per cent (Raine, 1993) to suggest that there is a genetic predisposition for crime.

However, these studies are purely correlational, showing as they do a connection between crime and biological characteristics by taking one variable and comparing it to another to see what the percentage likelihood of the two occurring together might be. Unfortunately, this does not show causation as it does not account for the range of other variables that may have come into play in determining a person's behaviour.

Furthermore, many of these studies have suffered from methodological problems related to the size of the sample, the identification of twin pairs as identical or not (judged by appearance rather than scientific tests), the fact that samples are sometimes chosen by identifying criminals and then going on to see if they have a twin who is also a criminal (confirmatory bias), the lack of control involved in adoption studies meaning that it is hard to make comparisons between biological and adoptive parents and the sometimes low percentages used to suggest the link between the two (Mednick et al., 1984).

The problem of causation is a major stumbling block in biological explanations as it brings into question the ability to say with any certainty that biological factors are anything more than just one risk factor in the range of factors that could be related to crime and given the low percentages, possibly not even a major factor.

The diathesis-stress model and crime

An answer to the problem of causation may come from the diathesis-stress model, which attempts to provide an interactionist explanation for crime with the biological factor (genetics, neural or even skull structure) providing the diathesis or predisposition towards crime and a social or psychological factor (child abuse, socialisation, personality or even just maternal deprivation) providing the stressful event that could act as the trigger for the predisposition to become exposed. Without the social/psychological trigger, it is unlikely that the individual will turn to crime, whatever their genes or brain/skull structure.

Raine (2002) has himself argued that those involved in research into biological causes need to be wary of not simply dismissing social factors as merely extraneous variables, otherwise they run the risk of ignoring very important factors that might not only help to explain the cause of the crime but also help with how the crime can be prevented.

However, Caspi et al. (2002) have taken this argument one step further with the evidence from their study that the specific genotype can mediate the influence of environmental factors. They found that the link between maltreatment in childhood was mediated by the activity of the MAOA gene such that those with low activity were likely to go on to show significant violence in adulthood, suggesting that the genotype can help to prevent the effect of environmental factors causing violent criminal behaviour in later life.

This suggests that the link between biology and crime, particularly violent crime is much more complicated than the simple association put forward by some of the biological explanations.

The question of racism and eugenics

One of the issues raised by most of these studies is what we can do with the information that we have. In other words, if we accept that biological factors such as genes or brain structure/activity are the cause then how can we prevent crime from occurring?

In some of the early gene studies mentioned in this chapter, Lange, 1929; Rosanoff, Handy and Rosanoff, 1934, the answer was fairly clear and they were, to varying degrees, considering the use of eugenics to deal with the problem and therefore potentially suggesting the use of sterilisation with certain groups in order to prevent the reproduction of violent and potentially criminal genes. Not long after the publication of Lange's work, the Nazi government in Germany passed the 'Law for the prevention of genetically diseased offspring' creating the possibility for the sterilisation of certain groups, which was supported by Lange. This conclusion was also supported by followers of Lombroso, for whom the prospect of being able to identify those with criminal characteristics and their associated gene pool offered the chance to use eugenics to defeat the problem of crime.

Unfortunately, a lot of this work is based on characteristics associated with certain ethnic groups such as those of African or Jewish origin and has been accused of providing a pseudo-scientific basis for racism. Even in modern times, similar arguments about the use of eugenics have tended to focus on minority ethnic groups due to their supposed heavier involvement with crime and have led some to argue for licences to allow some to reproduce while excluding others (Lykken, 1998).

The result of some of these ideas has been to unfairly and sometimes devastatingly (in the case of Nazi Germany) single out certain groups as needing to be controlled and possibly even removed from society in order that the genetically correct can be allowed to thrive and, in that way, we can do away with crime. Unfortunately, similar issues are now beginning to emerge in relation to studies into brain structure and activity, with studies showing that differences in the structure and activity of the amygdala in children as young as three was a predictor for adult criminality as it hampered their response to fear and made them less likely to fear the consequences of crime. Although such studies are not advocating eugenics, nor are they racist, they are suggesting treatment programmes aimed at changing these responses. This has led some to argue for brain scans to be used on all children to detect similar problems.

Think!

Do you think babies should have their brains scanned in order to find out if they are likely to commit crimes as an adult? If so, what do you think we should do with those that are found to have the wrong kind of brain?

What about polygenics?

One of the problems with putting forward the view that crime might have a genetic basis is the identification of a specific gene that is directly responsible for crime, something which has so far proved to be very difficult. Even the advocates of the influence of the MAOA gene aren't suggesting that it has a direct influence on crime but merely that it has an effect on an enzyme that in turn has an effect on neurotransmitters, which may have some influence on impulsive behaviour. This isn't exactly a gene for crime.

However, advances in the study of genetics have allowed the possibility of studying genome wide associations, which allow the possibility of identifying a number of genetic variants that may be associated with crime as well as determining if these variants are also linked to other traits.

In a meta-analysis of over 25,000 individuals taken from different regions to avoid overlap, Tielbeek et al. (2017), were able to show that the effect of individual genes on antisocial behaviour (ASB) was tiny but that the combined effect of a number of genes was significantly associated with ASB and importantly that the same polygenic effect was found for educational attainment, suggesting that there is a close association between crime and educational attainment at the genetic level.

However, the researchers were quick to point out that the polygenic influence on crime is only one factor and that other environmental factors, such as traumatic experiences during early years are at least as influential and have also pointed to the influence of epigenetics on gene expression as a factor that requires further study if we are going to provide a complete understanding of the causes of crime.

Mini plenary

Consider the arguments made above, both for and against the use of biological ideas/evidence to explain offending behaviour. What do you think? Use a separate sheet of paper to create a plan of the arguments for and against. Then, in no more than 100 words, explain whether we should use biological explanations for offending behaviour.

Arguments for	Arguments against

34

BIOLOGICAL EXPLANATIONS OF OFFENDING BEHAVIOUR

A modern issue: do biological explanations take away responsibility from the criminal?

One of the issues raised by these biological explanations for crime is to what extent they can take away blame from those who commit crimes. After all, if someone is 'born to kill', should we be surprised when they go on to kill someone? Furthermore, is it their fault, as after all, there was nothing they could do to change the brain they were born with.

New research

Jon Schuppe, Blame my brain: A killer's bold defense gets a court hearing. nbcnews.com, 27 April 2019.

In the article, Schuppe reports on the case of Anthony Blas Yepez, who was convicted of the murder of a 75-year-old man who he admitted he had beaten to death in a fit of rage. However, his defence lawyer (Ian Lloyd) has argued that Yepez should not be held responsible due to the fact that he had a rare genetic abnormality that meant he was unable to control his rage.

Schuppe reports on the increasing tendency in criminal cases for lawyers to use a defence based around behavioural genetics and neuroscience including reference to chemical imbalances and tumours.

In fact, Lloyd had only discovered the existence of the gene when he coincidentally attended a conference in Washington in which forensic scientist, William Bernet, had referred to another case in Tennessee (Bradley Waldroup) in which the defendant had avoided the death penalty partially due to his argument that he had a variant of the MAOA gene.

Having initially relied on home testing to show that Yepez had the same genetic mutation, Lloyd was later able to call on expert witnesses to testify that Yepez did indeed have the gene. Further evidence was brought forward to show that Yepez had also suffered extreme child abuse, which may have interacted with the gene to lead to his terrible behaviour.

The evidence was enough to enable Yepez to take his case to the supreme court but in the end, it didn't lead to any change in his conviction nor in his sentence, which was twenty-two and a half years in jail for second degree murder.

However, the article does refer to research conducted by Nita Farahany (2016) showing that between 2005 and 2015 there had been 2,800 cases in which neuroscience had been used as part of the defence and in 20 per cent of cases, the defendants had received a favourable outcome of some sort.

Question time

What does this article tell us about the causes of crime?

Do you think Yepez was responsible for his crime?

Should he have been charged in exactly the same way as every other criminal or he should he have been found not guilty by reason of an uncontrollable brain?

Chapter plenary

1. What is the historical approach to crime?
2. What is the atavistic form?
3. What are genetic explanations for crime?
4. What is involved in twin and adoption studies?
5. Is there a criminal gene?
6. What are the neural explanations for crime?
7. How does the idea of genotype and phenotype apply to crime?
8. What is the problem of causation in relation to studies of crime?
9. What is the diathesis-stress model of crime?
10. Why do biological explanations raise the question of racism and eugenics?
11. How does the idea of polygenics apply to crime?
12. Can we blame someone's brain for their crime?

Glossary

Key word	Definition
Amygdala	An almond-shaped mass of grey matter inside each cerebral hemisphere, involved with the experiencing of emotions.
Antisocial personality disorder	A mental condition where a person shows no regard for the rights or feelings of others (synonymous with psychopathy).
Candidate genes	Specific genes that may be responsible for criminal behaviour.
Concordance rates	The percentage likelihood of both twins sharing the same disorder or behaviour.
Corpus callosum	A broad band of nerve fibres joining the two hemispheres of the brain.
Diathesis-stress model	An explanation that focuses on the interaction between genes and experiences.

Key word	Definition
Dopamine	A neurotransmitter that plays a role in pleasure, motivation and learning.
DZ twins	Non-identical twins that have been formed from two separate eggs or zygotes.
Eugenics	A set of beliefs that it is possible to improve the genetic quality of the population by excluding certain genetic groups.
Genome wide associations	Studies that use gene mapping to identify genetic variations in a particular population.
Heritability	The likelihood that something is going to be inherited.
Human genome project	An international scientific research project to chart the entire genetic material of a human being, completed in 2003.
Instrumental aggression	Violent or aggressive acts that serve to get someone what they want.
MAOA	An enzyme that is involved in the regulation of serotonin, dopamine and noradrenaline.
Maternal deprivation	Having the bond between a baby and mother broken in the first two to three years of life, which has been linked to delinquency in later life.
MZ twins	Identical twins that have been formed from a single egg or zygote.
Noradrenaline	A hormone that acts as a neurotransmitter and is involved in the fight or flight response.
Parietal cortex	The outer layer of the parietal lobe, which is involved in the experience of touch and pain.
PET scans	A brain scan using a radioactive dye, which attaches itself to the active parts of the brain showing which parts are active at certain times.
Polygenic	The idea that criminal behaviour may be influenced by two or more genes.
Prefrontal cortex	The outer layer of the front part of the frontal lobe, which has been implicated in planning complex cognitive behaviour, personality expression, decision making and moderating social behaviour.
Serotonin	A neurotransmitter believed to be involved in the feeling of well-being or happiness.
Warrior gene	A gene that is responsible for violent and aggressive tendencies in a person.

Plenary: Exam-style questions and answers with advisory comments

Question 1.

Outline how the atavistic form can explain offending behaviour.   [2 marks]

Marks for this question: AO1 = 2

Advice: In a question like this, it's important to make sure you are clearly outlining the definition of this term and how it relates to offending behaviour. One way to do this is to provide a relevant example to help you. There is no need to provide any analysis or evaluation as both of the marks are for AO1: Knowledge and understanding.

Possible answer: This is a term used by Lombroso to describe someone who is a throwback to some form of primitive being that is somewhere between human and ape. Lombroso suggested that this being would be prone to criminal behaviour and could be identified by certain facial characteristics, such as a protruding jaw and sloping forehead.

Question 2.

Describe and evaluate genetic and/or neural explanations of offending.   **[16 marks]**

Marks for this question: AO1 = 6 and AO3 = 10

Advice: This question is looking for both skills of knowledge and understanding and analysis and evaluation. As there are 6 marks for AO1 and 10 for AO3, there should be greater emphasis on the evaluation. However, all such extended writing questions are marked holistically and therefore it is important that the knowledge is accurate and detailed and that the evaluation is clear and effective.

This question asks about two different approaches using the command of and/or, which means that you need to make a decision about whether to just focus on one in lots of detail or both in less detail. There will need to be a breadth/depth trade-off as just doing one will require more depth and doing two will require greater breadth.

Possible answer: There have been many attempts to identify a gene for criminal behaviour, all of which have found it very difficult to identify a single gene that could be shown to be responsible for crime. However, some have identified genes that may be responsible for violent crime due to their link with aggression, so-called candidate genes.

One such gene is the MAOA gene, which is involved in the regulation of serotonin, dopamine and noradrenaline and it has been found that deficiencies in this gene are associated with aggression, which could push some towards violent crime. Other studies have found a more direct link between the gene and crime leading to the use of the term, warrior gene, to describe those with this abnormality.

The influence of genes on behaviour has been studied by both twin studies and adoption studies. Twin studies are done because MZ twins are the only genetically identical individuals on the planet and if we can show that both sets of identical twins have the same tendencies towards criminal behaviour then we can go some way to showing that offending is genetic, particularly if the concordance rates for them are higher than they are for DZ twins.

Neural explanations are focused on the structure and activity of the brain to identify if there are differences in these areas between criminals and non-criminals, which might help to explain the differences in behaviour between the two groups.

As mentioned above, the genes that regulate serotonin, dopamine and noradrenaline are involved in aggression and violence, so it would seem reasonable to suggest that these neurotransmitters are involved in the production of aggression and therefore could be related to violent crime. Research by Raine et al. using PET scans showed that there was reduced activity in the prefrontal cortex of 41 criminals compared to a matched control group of 41 non-criminals. They also found activity differences in other areas of the brain suggesting that there may be a number of differences in brain activity that contribute to violent crime. In a later study, Raine found an 11 per cent reduction in the volume of grey matter in the PFC of subjects with antisocial personality disorder, suggesting that this part of the brain, which is particularly involved in the control of impulsive behaviour, may help to explain the behaviour of violent criminals.

One of the issues with biological explanations for offending is that a lot of the evidence for the biological causes of crime comes from studies that intend to show an association between crime and some other variable, be it genes or brain structure and brain activity. Twin studies have been able to show concordance rates of around 50 per cent to suggest that there is a genetic predisposition for crime. However, these studies are purely correlational, showing as they do a connection between crime and biological characteristics by taking one variable and comparing it to another to see what the percentage likelihood of the two occurring together might be. Unfortunately, this does not show causation as it does not account for the range of other variables that may have come into play in determining a person's behaviour.

An answer to the problem of causation may come from the diathesis-stress model, which attempts to provide an interactionist explanation for crime with the biological factor (genetics, neural or even skull structure) providing the diathesis or predisposition towards crime and a social or psychological factor (child abuse, socialisation or even personality) providing the stressful event that could act as the trigger for the predisposition to become exposed. Without the social/psychological trigger then it is unlikely that the individual will turn to crime, whatever their genes or brain/skull structure.

Raine has himself argued that those involved in research into biological causes need to be wary of not simply dismissing social factors as merely extraneous variables, otherwise they run the risk of ignoring very important factors that might not only help to explain the cause of the crime but also help with how the crime can be prevented.

One of the issues raised by most of these studies is what we can do with the information that we have. In other words, if we accept that biological factors such as genes or brain structure/activity are the cause then how can we prevent crime from occurring?

Unfortunately, some of the past work on biological factors have led to the idea of eugenics and trying to get rid of people with certain characteristics so that society can be crime free and some of this has focused on racial differences and characteristics. Even in modern times, similar arguments about the use of eugenics have tended to focus on minority ethnic groups due to their supposed heavier involvement with crime, which could leave these explanations open to claims of racism.

Unfortunately, similar issues are now beginning to emerge in relation to studies into brain structure and activity, with studies showing that differences in the structure and activity of the amygdala in children as young as three was a predictor for adult criminality as it hampered their response to fear and made them less likely to fear the consequences of crime. Although such studies are not advocating eugenics, nor are they racist, they are suggesting treatment programmes aimed at changing these responses. This has led some to argue for brain scans to be used on all children to detect similar problems, which seems highly unethical and possibly even dangerous.

The final issue here is to what extent this research might be used to shift blame away from the criminals themselves, as if we can blame their behaviour on their brain structure or activity or even their genes, then surely they can't be held responsible for their behaviour. This poses difficult questions for the legal system and for the rest of society, which is likely to be increasing with the increased use of technology to detect these differences.

References

Brunner, H.G., Nelen, M.R., Van Zandvoort, P., Abeling, N.G., Van Gennip, A.H., Wolters, E.C., Kuiper, M.A., Ropers, H.H. and Van Oost, B.A. (1993) X-linked borderline mental retardation with prominent behavioral disturbance: Phenotype, genetic localization, and evidence for disturbed monoamine metabolism. American Journal of Human Genetics, 52(6): 1032.

Caspi, A., McClay, J., Moffitt, T.E., Mill, J., Martin, J., Craig, I.W., Taylor, A. and Poulton, R. (2002) Role of genotype in the cycle of violence in maltreated children. Science, 297(5582): 851–854.

Christiansen, K.O. (1977) A preliminary study of criminality among twins. In Mednick, S. A. and Christiansen, K. O. (eds.), Biosocial Bases of Criminal Behavior. New York: Gardner Press.

Farahany, N.A. (2016). Neuroscience and behavioral genetics in US criminal law: An empirical analysis. Journal of Law and the Biosciences, 2(3): 485–509.

Lange J. (1929). Verbrechen als Schicksal. Thieme, Leipzig (English edition; Unwin, London).

Lea, R. and Chambers, G. (2007) Monoamine oxidase, addiction, and the 'warrior' gene hypothesis. The New Zealand Medical Journal (Online), 120(1250).

Lombroso, C. (1911) Criminal Man, According to the Classification System of Caesare Lombroso. Ed. Gina Lombroso Ferrero. New York: GP Putnam's Sons, p. 191.

Lykken, D.T. (1998) The case for parental licensure. *Psychopathy: Antisocial, criminal, and violent behavior*, pp. 122–143.

Mednick S.A., Gabrielli W.F., Hutchings B. (1984) Genetic influences in criminal convictions: Evidence from an adoption cohort. *Science*, 224: 891–894.

Raine, A. (1993) *The Psychopathology of Crime: Criminal Behavior as a Clinical Disorder*. San Diego: Academic Press.

Raine, A., Buchsbaum, M. and LaCasse, L. (1997) Brain abnormalities in murderers indicated by positron emission tomography. *Biological psychiatry*, 42(6): 495–508.

Rosanoff, A.J., Handy, L.M. and Rosanoff, I.A. (1934). Criminality and delinquency in twins. *Journal of Criminal Law and Criminology* (1931–1951), 24(5): 923–934.

Tielbeek, J.J., Johansson, A., Polderman, T.J., Rautiainen, M.R., Jansen, P., Taylor, M., Tong, X., Lu, Q., Burt, A.S., Tiemeier, H. and Viding, E. (2017) Genome-wide association studies of a broad spectrum of antisocial behavior. *JAMA psychiatry*, 74(12): 1242–1250.

Tiihonen, J., Rautiainen, M.R., Ollila, H.M., Repo-Tiihonen, E., Virkkunen, M., Palotie, A., Pietiläinen, O., Kristiansson, K. et al. (2015). Genetic background of extreme violent behavior. Molecular psychiatry, 20(6): 786–792.

Chapter 4
Psychological explanations of offending behaviour 1 – Eysenck's theory of the criminal personality and differential association theory

Psychological explanations of offending behaviour: Eysenck's theory of the criminal personality; differential association theory.

AO1 (Knowledge and understanding): Psychological explanations of offending behaviour 1 – Eysenck's theory of criminal personality and differential association theory

Eysenck's view of personality

You've probably heard people say that they are a bit of an extravert or maybe that they are a bit introverted or even describe other people as slightly neurotic without properly understanding what these terms mean. In a psychological sense the terms are mostly associated with the work of Hans Eysenck (1947) who developed a theory of personality based around the notion that there are certain personality types that are spread across two dimensions, introversion/extraversion (E) and neuroticism/stability (N). These two dimensions were initially used to provide the basis of personality such that someone could be regarded as high or low on each dimension, e.g. highly extraverted and highly neurotic. In later years, a further dimension was added by Eysenck (1952), which was a measure of psychoticism (P) that would be expected to be low in most people, whereas the other two E and N would be expected to be more normally distributed.

The measurement of personality

Eysenck believed that it was possible to measure someone's personality using a self-report measure called the Eysenck Personality Questionnaire (EPQ), which would allow someone to be placed along a continuum of personality characteristics established from their score on this questionnaire.

Extraversion could be measured with questions like:

- Are you a talkative person?
- Do you often do things on the spur of the moment?

Those scoring high on the extraversion scale would be active and impulsive with those scoring low being quiet and reserved.

Neuroticism could be measured with questions like:

- Does your mood often go up and down?
- Are you an irritable person?

Those scoring high on the neuroticism scale would be anxious and moody with those scoring low being calm and even tempered.

Psychoticism would be measured with questions like:

- Do you enjoy hurting people you love?
- Would you like to think that people are afraid of you?

Those scoring high on this dimension would probably not be the kind of people you would like to meet!

Think!

Do these questions relate to the characteristics that they are intended to measure?

Do you think the responses to these questions would be entirely honest? Why?

The biological basis of personality

Eysenck's early work on psychiatry had led him down the path of looking at biological explanations for behaviour and he was particularly keen to try to understand the biological influences on our personality, as he believed that it would be reasonable to try to understand personality in relation to the constitutional make-up of a person. As we will see later, Eysenck did not deny the influence of environmental factors but felt that some researchers had gone too far in attempting to explain personality in relation to purely social or psychological factors.

Eysenck (1963) had noticed that different types of drugs would affect someone's position on the introversion/extraversion scale, such that stimulants would shift a person towards the introversion end and depressants would shift a person towards the extraversion end. As these drugs act upon the reticular activating system (RAS), Eysenck believed that it must be the activity in this part of the nervous system that is involved; hypothesising that those with low levels of activity and therefore low levels of arousal (extraverts) would seek out arousing activities in order to raise their cortical arousal to its optimum level. Those with already high levels of activity in this area and therefore high levels of arousal (introverts) would have no need to raise their levels of cortical arousal and would therefore have no need to seek out further stimulation. Eysenck believed that these different levels of activity would most probably have been inherited.

The criminal personality

In its most basic form, Eysenck regards extraversion as the most obvious dimension pushing people towards crime as this is likely to make a person sensation seeking. This is similar to Zuckerman (1983), who suggested that sensation seekers are risk-takers who seek out stimulation through activities that are potentially danger-ous but extremely stimulating; so some people might jump off a bridge with nothing but a piece of elasticated rope attached to their leg but others may steal a car for the thrill of being chased by the police!

Neuroticism also plays a part, as those high on this dimension would be more likely to react quickly and unpredictably leading to their behaviour being erratic and potentially placing them in situations where they are more likely to strike out when the environment is stressful or emotionally demanding. This could relate to criminal behaviour as it linked with uncontrolled aggressive behaviour.

Psychoticism also plays a significant part, as those scoring high on this dimension have significantly less concern for others and are mainly concerned with their own gratification – they could be aggressive towards others as they feel little or no con-science, similar to the psychopath. Those high on this scale would be most likely to commit acts that are antisocial as they have no regard for the feelings of others.

The role of conditioning

This theory is by no means all biological, as Eysenck (1960) was strongly influenced by the work of Pavlov on classical conditioning and was keen to point out the role of conditioning in relation to criminal behaviour. It was his contention that crim-inal or antisocial behaviour was conditioned in a similar way to other behaviour through the association between stimulus and response. Eysenck was keen to show how moral values could be learned through a process of associating a fear response to what are essentially natural impulses towards aggressive behaviour. Consequently, he was less interested in what made a child criminal (as it is natural) and more interested in what stopped a child from becoming criminal (as it is learned).

The connection with the dimensions of personality is that those with a naturally extravert personality were particularly unresponsive to conditioning so it would be much harder for them to form these associations that would help them to learn to control their impulses. The neurotic personality was more easily conditioned but combined with a high level of extraversion, the individual would be more likely to be conditioned into crime than out of it by their tendency to engage in behav-iour that might bring pleasure from the reward of sensation seeking or risk-taking. The psychotic dimension would be more likely to come into play later in life and although it wasn't completely clear what caused this to happen (Eysenck suggested that it may be polygenic), it is clear that such people could be much more dangerous due to their lack of feeling for others.

Eysenck's theory is therefore more of a biosocial theory as it combines the influence of biology and learning in the development of behaviour and in particular in the development of criminal behaviour. Criminal tendencies are modified both by the influence of society and by natural personality characteristics that push some people towards criminal behaviour, while at the same time making them resistant to measures to change their behaviour.

Question time

What parts of Eysenck's theory are psychological? What parts are biological? Do you think it is more of one than the other? Why?
Is there anything missing from this theory? If so, what?

How does differential association theory explain crime?

At some point in your life, you may have had someone warn you about the dangers of hanging around with certain people, for example, your parents may have told you not to do it as they feared you would pick up some bad habits and get into trouble just by associating with the wrong people. This is the basis of differential association theory as it attempts to explain the involvement in criminal behaviour by looking at the kind of people we associate with.

According to Sutherland (1939), crime is a learned behaviour, which is learned in much the same way as many other forms of behaviour, through the interaction with significant others whose values can be picked up in the process of learning. This is not the same as saying that the behaviour of others is imitated in a kind of social learning manner but that learning is more indirect with an effect on the motivation for crime.

An excess of pro-crime attitudes

Most people come into contact with both pro-crime attitudes and anti-crime attitudes from the people that they come into contact with. Each of these types of people will have their own ideas or ways of defining what is and isn't appropriate. If we come into contact with more pro-crime attitudes then we will end up with an excess of such attitudes, which in turn is likely to have the effect of making us favour those kind of attitudes: it's a simple matter of maths!

The contact with pro-crime attitudes and isolation from anti-crime attitudes is likely to occur due to the different individuals or groups that we associate with and these associations will develop through the normal process of socialisation.

Criminal techniques

The other part of this theory is the idea that in these associations we are likely to learn things other than just norms and values and we will also be exposed to ideas about the techniques required to commit criminal acts. Just as someone exposed to non-criminal values might learn a variety of skills and techniques associated with non-criminal behaviour, so those exposed to criminal values might also learn about criminal techniques, like how to break into a car.

This relates closely to the notion of universities of crime (explored in more depth in Chapter 7) in which those going to prison come into contact with a whole range of criminals who have been involved in a whole range of crimes and as a result pick up new ideas for how to commit crime. This can happen through the normal process of socialisation.

Question time

How does differential association theory explain crime?

Does this apply to real life? Why/not?

Mini plenary

Without referring back to the text, explain the difference between Eysenck's theory and differential association theory in no more than 50 words.

_____

_____

_____

_____

_____

_____

_____

AO2 (Application of knowledge): How does this apply in practice?

Interleave me now

The nature-nurture debate

The extent to which behaviour is affected by factors that are present at birth or by environmental factors that occur after birth is the subject of the nature-nurture debate and is one of the oldest debates in the whole of psychology. Some would argue that nature is more important, as all our behaviour is ultimately governed by our brain and nervous system, however, others would argue that nurture is more important, as our behaviour is conditioned by environmental factors that occur as we encounter new experiences.

Nature-nurture and crime

The debate over nature and nurture has received particular focus in the field of murder, with continued interest in the question of whether some people are born to kill. The debate has come to a head due to the fact that some murderers appear to have no particular experiences/associations in their lives that would explain how they came to do the crime they did. Although it seems ridiculous to argue that some people might have life experiences that would push them towards murder, it is undoubtedly the case that some people do have terrible experiences/associations that might help to explain why they are murderers. Caspi et al. (2002) provide some evidence for this argument in their study that showed how the predisposition towards violence might be triggered by maltreatment in childhood, however, some people become violent with no obvious experience of such abuse (see Table 4.1).

Table 4.1 Ted Bundy – born to kill?

Ted Bundy was the all-American boy next door, just the sort of man your parents would be happy for you to bring home. He was from a good family, he was good-looking and he had good prospects as he was studying for a law degree. Bundy was outgoing, friendly and highly sociable. However, Bundy was in fact one of the most notorious serial killers in American history, having been convicted of the murder of at least 30 women. He was described by some as being 'the very definition of heartless evil' and even described himself as 'the most cold-hearted son of a bitch you'll ever meet'.

What made him become this is still a mystery. Was it just the fact that he was born that way? Why was he able to hide it so well that when he was arrested, few that knew him could believe that he was responsible. One of his co-workers on a suicide hotline that he volunteered for described him as 'kind and empathetic'. Was he just born to kill?

Think!

What do you think? Could it have just been in Bundy's nature to kill?

Are there clues to his crime in his personality?

Are there any other factors that could explain his behaviour?

Mini plenary

Kris is a very active person who is always on the lookout for new activities that he can get involved in because he gets really bored by just sitting at home watching TV. Jay, on the other hand, is quite happy to stay at home and read a good book; he doesn't need a lot of action in his life, as he gets quite enough stimulation at home.

Using Eysenck's theory, explain which one out of Kris and Jay is more likely to become involved in crime and why.

_____

_____

_____

_____

_____

_____

_____

_____

_____

AO3 (Analysis and evaluation of knowledge): How useful are these explanations for crime?

Evidence for Eysenck's explanation

The connection between personality type and crime should be relatively easy to test as, if we identify those that have been involved in crime and then employ Eysenck's personality questionnaire with these individuals, then we should be able to see if the connection is there, particularly if we also use a control group of non-criminals to compare to.

Center and Kemp (2002) took this approach with a meta-analysis of 11 studies that had attempted to find a link between antisocial behaviour (ASB) and personality type. The studies all involved the use of children or adolescents who had been involved in some form of ASB and all of whom had been tested on Eysenck's three dimensions, using some form of Eysenck's personality questionnaire (EPQ) and the studies all had a control group who either had no evidence of behavioural problems or who had been referred for problems unrelated to ASB.

They found a significant association between ASB and psychoticism, which is important as they believed this was a significant characteristic pushing someone towards ASB, however, they found no significant association between extraversion or neuroticism and ASB, which they had suggested would have been important to provide evidence in favour of Eysenck's explanation.

This study suggested that the tendency towards the psychotic or psychopathic characteristic is an important factor in crime and this has been shown in relation to a number of other explanations, e.g. Bowlby's maternal deprivation hypothesis, but they did not find support for the other dimensions, suggesting that they don't have the effect proposed by Eysenck.

Center and Kemp did recognise that Eysenck had suggested that other environmental/learning factors do play an important part in the development of criminal tendencies and ASB, which they had not looked at in this study but according to Eysenck these factors will only be important for those individuals that have the relevant personality types, so again it seems as though his explanation lacks validity.

The implications for the treatment of offenders

The notion of personality type and in particular the notion that it has a biological foundation could lead to the conclusion that it is extremely difficult or impossible to do anything about crime and Eysenck (1960) himself has commented that it would be very difficult to treat a criminal with the use of traditional methods of punishment or deterrence, as the lack of responsiveness to conditioning would mean that such individuals would not be put off by such methods.

Eysenck argues that the form of treatment for each individual should be tailored to their specific needs as their response to the form of treatment will depend on their individual personality as measured by the EPQ and to some extent their individual experiences. If there were to be a general response to the problem, Eysenck suggested that it might involve use of the drugs referred to earlier, e.g. stimulants being given to those with an extravert personality – as they would then presumably not need to seek stimulation through crime.

This would of course be very difficult to implement, as the idea of having individual treatment programmes for criminals would be both financially and politically expensive for any government who put the idea forward. Furthermore, neither of these suggestions deal with the fact that those high in psychoticism are notoriously difficult to treat. Rahman and Eysenck (1978) found that those who score high on the P scale were difficult to treat due to their hostility and paranoia, suggesting that the usefulness of this approach is at best severely limited and at worst impossible to implement due to the cost and likely backlash from the public if it were to be put into practice.

Think!

Do you think it would be a good idea to treat those identified as extraverts with stimulants to prevent them from turning to crime?

How do you think we would be able to identify them? Can you see any problems with this procedure?

Are drug treatments the way forward for the treatment of criminality?

The possibility of cultural bias in the explanation

One of the issues raised by theories such as these is the extent to which they can be applied cross-culturally, particularly as they were developed in western individualistic cultures and may not therefore be as applicable to eastern collectivist cultures. It could be that personality factors are more of an issue in individualistic cultures due to their focus on individual differences and therefore it may be that there is a bias towards over-representing one's own individuality on questionnaires such as that used by Eysenck, which might not appear in other collectivist cultures.

Sikand and Reddy (2017) attempted to study the role of psychosocial factors in the criminal behaviour of adults in India with a particular focus on the three dimensions P, E and N. They used the EPQ-R with 20 individuals who had a criminal record and a group of 20 non-criminals matched on age, gender and socioeconomic status. They found no differences on any of the three dimensions, suggesting that personality type was not a factor in their crimes, finding instead that lack of social support, lack of focus on education and financial constraints were of more significance for this particular group.

This seems to suggest that in a culture that is very different from the culture in which Eysenck's theory was developed, the effect of personality type is not a significant influence on crime. However, this was quite a small sample and in a similar study also conducted in India by Bathla and Kaur (2014) with 200 convicts, they did find that these individuals scored particularly high on a measure of neuroticism, although in that study there was no control group and they were using a different measure of neuroticism (five factor model) from that used by Eysenck.

Is differential association enough for crime to occur?

Alternative theories of the turn to crime have been suggested and one that is particularly relevant to this discussion is social control theory, which suggests that the decision to engage in criminal behaviour is based on the kind of relationships and commitments that bond people to their society, which serve to hold them back from any natural tendencies that might push someone towards criminal behaviour.

Church et al. (2009) argue that the tendency towards criminal behaviour comes about from a combination of these approaches, in that differential association explains the motivation for crime and social control explains how crime is kept going. Consequently, it is the combination of the two that provides the full explanation for crime and one without the other wouldn't be enough.

Church et al. used self-report scales to identify factors like family stressors and their peers' delinquent activity and found that apart from these general theories, the specific factor that had the biggest effect on the likelihood of criminal behaviour was family stressors such as divorce, loss of jobs, serious illness or death in the family.

Once again, this suggests that the general idea of differential association isn't enough on its own to explain crime and that there are specific social factors that play a major part in the push towards criminal behaviour.

Is the questionnaire method an adequate measure of personality or differential association?

The question of the usefulness of questionnaires has a long history in psychology with many questions being raised as to their validity and the problem of social desirability bias, not to mention the issue of whether different questionnaires are measuring the same thing. Furthermore, it may be that personality or associations are difficult to measure in terms of a single score – it may be that they are much more sophisticated than that and require a much more detailed and possibly more individual form of measurement.

Many of these issues are incompatible because if you were to come up with a more individualised measure then it would be impossible to compare and virtually impossible to consider whether you are measuring the same thing. Consequently, it may be useful to consider the methods used to measure antisocial behaviour and crime, as this may have questionable validity depending on whether it is based on actual convictions or self-reports.

Farrington (1992) has suggested that the connection between neuroticism/extraversion and crime may depend on how the data on criminal behaviour is gathered, as he found that if the data was taken from official records of convictions then the measure of personality was different from those individuals for whom the data had been gathered by self-reports. The finding was that the official criminals scored low on the extraversion scale but high on the neuroticism scale, whereas for the self-reported criminals the score was high on the extraversion scale and low on the neuroticism scale.

There could also be a problem when measuring variables such as family stressors/family cohesion or even associations and relationships with other people (differential associations) as people may not want to reveal everything about the relationships with their families and friends and may therefore give socially desirable answers that don't represent reality.

This suggests that the relationship between Eysenck's dimensions and crime is difficult to reliably establish, with similar problems affecting the study of differential associations, meaning that the use of self-reports in this process may bring into question the validity of the data collected.

Mini plenary

In the table below, outline the arguments for/against both Eysenck's theory and differential association theory.

Theory	Arguments for	Arguments against
Eysenck's theory		
Differential association theory		

A modern issue: can differential associations be applied to social media?

One of the issues facing society today is the problematic use of social media, with groups putting forwards racist and xenophobic views as well as groups promoting and supporting acts of terror and mass murder. The question considered here is whether such behaviour can be explained by the same differential associations that can be applied to other forms of crime.

New research

James Hawdon (2012). Applying differential association theory to online hate groups: a theoretical statement, Center for Peace Studies and Violence Prevention, Virginia Tech.

In the article, Hawdon attempts to apply some of the core ideas of differential association theory (DAT) to the involvement in online hate groups. Hawdon works through what he sees as some of these core principles first and then tries to show how they may explain some of this behaviour.

Firstly, he argues that DAT suggests that crime is learned though communicative interaction and there is little more on the planet that works on the basis of communicative interaction than social media. Secondly, he argues that DAT suggests that crime is learned though intimate personal relationships and for many young people this would include all the people that are their 'friends' on social media.

Thirdly, with regard to the techniques for crime being learned from others, he argues that there are numerous examples of hate crime being espoused on social media, which it is very easy for someone who spends a lot of time online to come across.

This leads on to the fourth principle, which concerns the pro-crime ideas exceeding the anti-crime ideas and while Hawdon accepts that there are many more anti-hate crime messages in normal life. It could be that spending so much time on social media builds up a potential for excess but also that the intensity of these messages may make them more of a powerful influence than the messages that go against them.

According to Hawdon, the internet provides people with access to messages of hate that they may not come across in their everyday lives, but on the web, there could be masses of them and if someone ventures into one or two of these and maybe even searches for them then Hawdon argues they can be caught up in a filter bubble.

The filter bubble is related to the use of algorithms by companies like Google that tailor your searches to things you seem to be interested in, so once you venture into the world of online hate, there may be more things presented to you that are similar. This would increase your access to these kinds of views and then lead on to you having an excess of these in comparison to anti-hate views.

For Hawdon, this is a dangerous process that could lead a person into associations that potentially influence their involvement in similar activities and the resulting criminality that goes with it.

Question time

What does this article tell us about the relationship between differential associations and hate crime?

Do you think that simply being exposed to these ideas on the internet may encourage someone to get involved?

What could be done to prevent this happening? Who would be responsible for preventing this?

Chapter plenary

1. What is Eysenck's view of personality?
2. How does Eysenck measure personality?
3. What is the biological basis of personality according to Eysenck?
4. What is the personality of a criminal according to Eysenck?
5. What is the role of conditioning in Eysenck's theory?
6. What is meant by differential association?
7. How does the idea of an excess of pro-crime attitudes relate to crime?
8. How are criminal techniques learned?
9. What is the nature-nurture debate?
10. How does nature and nurture apply to these two theories?
11. What is the evidence for Eysenck's theory?
12. What are the implications of Eysenck's theory for the treatment of offenders?
13. How does the idea of cultural bias apply to Eysenck's theory?
14. What are the alternatives to differential association theory?
15. Is the questionnaire method an adequate way of measuring personality or differential associations?
16. Can differential associations be applied to the issue of hate-crime in social media?

Glossary

Key word	Definition
Anti-crime attitudes	Opinions that are negatively directed towards the idea of crime.
Biosocial theory	An explanation for behaviour that combines biological explanations with social/psychological explanations.

Key word	Definition
Bowlby's maternal deprivation hypothesis	Separation from your mother in early childhood will lead to delinquency in later life.
Classical conditioning	A form of learning whereby a **conditioned** stimulus (CS) becomes associated with an unrelated unconditioned stimulus (US) in order to produce a behavioural response known as a **conditioned** response (CR).
Collectivist cultures	A type of society where the focus is on the needs of the group.
Constitutional make-up	The physical make-up of someone's body including the biological processes that govern someone's reaction to stimuli.
EPQ	The questionnaire used by Eysenck to measure the different types of personality.
EPQ-R	A revised version of the EPQ, which was used later by Eysenck and others testing his theory.
Extraversion	A personality type that is outward looking and needs a lot of stimulation.
Individualistic cultures	A type of society where the focus is on the needs of the individual.
Introversion	A personality type that is inward looking and reserved and needs very little stimulation.
Meta-analysis	A method of research using data from a number of previous studies to try to establish an overall trend.
Neuroticism	A tendency to be anxious and self-doubting and experiencing a lot of negative feelings.
Pro-crime attitudes	Opinions that are positively directed towards the idea of crime.
Psychoticism	A tendency to be hostile and aggressive to others as there is a lack of empathy and concern for others.
Reticular activating system (RAS)	A bundle of nerves at our brainstem that filters out unnecessary information so the important stuff gets through. Your RAS takes what you focus on and creates a filter for it. It then sifts through the data and presents only the pieces that are important to you.
Socialisation	Features of the external world that may affect our behaviour as we grow and develop, including other people, social situations and experiences.

Plenary: Exam-style questions and answers with advisory comments

Question 1.

Briefly explain Eysenck's theory of the criminal personality. [3 marks]

Marks for this question: AO1 = 3

Advice: In a question like this, it's important to make sure you are explaining the theory, so this will require a little more detail but it also needs to be fairly brief as it is only 3 marks. There is no need to provide any analysis or evaluation as all of the marks are for AO1: Knowledge and understanding.

Possible answer: Eysenck believed that there were two basic measures of personality, introversion vs extraversion and neuroticism vs stability. Neurotic extraverts would be more likely to turn to criminal behaviour as the extravert part of the personality would seek out highly stimulating behaviour due to the low activity of their reticular activating system. The neurotic part of the personality would make them behave in an unpredictable and impulsive manner, which could make them respond quickly to certain situations. The final part of the criminal personality was psychoticism, which led the person to have no feelings for others and the three of these combined might make the person more likely to carry out criminal activities such as theft.

Question 2.

Discuss the differential association theory of offending behaviour. Refer to at least one other explanation of offending behaviour in your answer. [16 marks]

Marks for this question: AO1 = 6 and AO3 = 10

Advice: This question asks for at least two explanations of offending to be considered. Although there should be a strong emphasis on differential association theory, there will need to be some significant mention of one other theory, which could be Eysenck's theory.

This question is looking for both skills of knowledge and understanding and analysis and evaluation. As there are 6 marks for AO1 and 10 for AO3, there should be greater emphasis on the evaluation. However, all such extended writing questions are marked holistically and therefore it is important that the knowledge is accurate and detailed and that the evaluation is clear and effective.

Possible answer: At some point in your life, you may have had someone warn you about the dangers of hanging around with certain people, for example, your parents may have told you not to do it as they feared you would pick up some bad habits and get into trouble just by associating with the wrong people. This is the basis of differential association theory as it attempts to explain the involvement in criminal behaviour by looking at the kind of people we associate with.

According to Sutherland (1939), crime is a learned behaviour, which is learned in much the same way as many other forms of behaviour, through the interaction with significant others and the values that significant others hold can be picked up in the process of learning.

Most people come into contact with both **pro-crime attitudes** and **anti-crime attitudes** from the people they come into contact with. Each of these types of people will have their own ideas or ways of defining what is and isn't appropriate. If we come into contact with more pro-crime attitudes, then we will end up with an excess of such attitudes, which in turn is likely to have the effect of making us favour those kind of attitudes: it's a simple matter of maths!

The contact with pro-crime attitudes and isolation from anti-crime attitudes is likely to occur due to the different individuals or groups that we associate with and these associations will develop through the normal process of **socialisation**.

The other part of this theory is the idea that in these associations we are likely to learn things other than just norms and values. We will also be exposed to ideas about the techniques required to commit criminal acts. Just as someone exposed to non-criminal values might learn a variety of skills and techniques associated with non-criminal behaviour, so those exposed to criminal values might also learn about criminal techniques, like how to break into a car.

Alternative theories of the turn to crime have been suggested and one that is particularly relevant to this discussion is social control theory, which suggests that the decision to engage in criminal behaviour is based on the kind of relationships and commitments that bond people to their society, which serve to hold them back from any natural tendencies that might push someone towards criminal behaviour.

Church et al. (2009) argue that the tendency towards criminal behaviour comes about from a combination of these approaches, in that differential association explains the motivation for crime and social control explains how crime is kept going. Consequently, it is the combination of the two that provides the full explanation for crime and one without the other wouldn't be enough.

Another theory that might help explain the motivation towards crime is Eysenck's theory of the criminal personality. Eysenck believed that neurotic extraverts would be more likely to turn to criminal behaviour, as the extravert part of the personality would seek out highly stimulating behaviour due to the low activity of their reticular activating system. The neurotic part of the personality would make them behave in an unpredictable and impulsive manner, which could make them respond quickly to certain situations. The final part of the criminal personality was psychoticism, which led the person to have no feelings for others. It is the combination of these three parts of the personality that pushes people towards crime rather than just the other people they associate with.

Church et al. used self-report scales to identify factors like family stressors and their peers' delinquent activity and found that apart from these general theories, the specific factor that had the biggest effect on the likelihood of criminal behaviour was family stressors such as divorce, loss of jobs, serious illness or death in the family.

Once again, this suggests that the general idea of differential association isn't enough on its own to explain crime and that there are specific social or personality factors that play a major part in the push towards criminal behaviour.

However, one of the problems with all the theories described in this chapter is that they have all used self-report techniques to identify the motivation for criminal behaviour and this may be a questionable technique when trying to get to the heart of the truth behind someone's behaviour.

This could be a particular problem when trying to measure factors such as family stressors/family cohesion or even your associations and relationships with other people (differential associations), as people may not want to reveal everything about the relationships with their families and friends and may therefore give socially desirable answers that don't represent reality.

This has also been problematic with Eysenck's theory as Farrington found differences in the questionnaire scores of those who had been convicted of offences from those who were simply self-reporting their history of crime, such that the 'official' criminals actually scored low on the extraversion scale but high on the neuroticism scale, whereas for the self-reported criminals the score was high on the extraversion scale and low on the neuroticism scale. This suggests that that the use of self-reports in the process of trying to understand offending behaviour may lack validity.

References

Bathla, A. and Kaur, K. (2014). A study of psychological variables and subjective well-being among convicts of Punjab. *Indian Journal of Health and Wellbeing*, 5(5): 545.

Center, D.B. and Kemp, D.E. (2002). Antisocial behaviour in children and Eysenck's theory of personality: An evaluation. *International Journal of Disability, Development and Education*, 49(4): 353–366.

Church, W.T., Wharton, T. and Taylor, J.K. (2009). An examination of differential association and social control theory: Family systems and delinquency. *Youth Violence and Juvenile Justice*, 7(1): 3–15.

Eysenck, H.J. (1947). *Dimensions of Personality*. London: Routledge & Kegan Paul; New York: Praeger.

Eysenck, H.J. (1952). *The Scientific Study of Personality*. Macmillan: New York.

Eysenck, H.J. (1960). Symposium: The development of moral values in children: VII – The Contribution of Learning Theory. *British Journal of Educational Psychology*, 30(1): 11–21.

Eysenck, H. (1963). Biological basis of personality. *Nature*, 199: 1031–1034.

Farrington, D.P. (1992). Explaining the beginning, progress, and ending of antisocial behaviour from birth to adulthood. *Facts, Frameworks, and Forecasts*, 3: 253–286.

Hawdon, J.E. (2012). Applying differential association theory to online hate groups: A theoretical statement. *Research on Finnish Society Vol. 5*, pp. 39–47.

Rahman, M.A. and Eysenck, S.B.G. (1978). Psychoticism and response to treatment in neurotic patients. *Behaviour Research and Therapy*, 16(3): 183–189.

Sikand, M. and Reddy, K.J. (2017). Role of psychosocial factors in criminal behaviour in adults in India. *International Journal of Criminal Justice Sciences*, 12(1).

Sutherland, Edwin H. (1939). *Principles of Criminology*, 3rd edn. Philadelphia: Lippincott.

Zuckerman, M. (ed.) (1983). *Biological Bases of Sensation Seeking, Impulsivity, and Anxiety*. Lawrence Erlbaum Associates.

Chapter 5
Psychological explanations of offending behaviour 2 – Cognitive explanations

Spec check

Psychological explanations of offending behaviour cognitive explanations: level of moral reasoning and cognitive distortions, including hostile attribution bias and minimalisation.

AO1 (Knowledge and understanding): Psychological explanations of offending behaviour 2 – cognitive explanations

The cognitive explanation of offending

In the introduction to this book, the question of what is a crime was considered, with the possibility put forward that crime is a relative concept based on circumstantial factors. One of these factors could be whether someone thinks that what they are doing is right or wrong and how they make sense of situations that could lead them into criminal behaviour. The focus of cognitive explanations is on the mind and how mental processes operate to help us make sense of what is right and wrong, rather than necessarily on some fixed and unchanging notion of morality.

The cognitive explanations presented in this chapter can be divided into two camps: one focuses on how the level of moral reasoning develops in stages and changes throughout life into a more mature and sophisticated understanding of what is right and wrong; the other focuses on how we attempt to process the information that is presented to us on a daily basis and how this can become distorted leading to us behaving in an antisocial manner.

What is Kohlberg's view of the level of moral reasoning?

Stage theories of cognitive development have often been associated with the work of Piaget, who believed that children move through stages as they grow older that are qualitatively different from one another. In relation to moral development, this means that a child's understanding of what is right and wrong would be different depending on their stage of development, with a full understanding being completed at around the age of nine or ten.

Kohlberg uses a similar stage approach to the understanding of moral development by arguing that moral reasoning develops in levels, with each level having a slightly different understanding of what is right and wrong. The higher the level, the more mature and sophisticated our understanding of right and wrong becomes. Unlike Piaget, Kohlberg wasn't suggesting that these levels would fit with a particular age but that they would fit with different levels of sophistication in the thinking of an individual. Therefore, it may be that younger children are more likely to be at the lower levels but it could be that older children and adults could also be at this level, which might explain their involvement with crime. Each level has two substages that have an orientation or particular focus on certain principles that drive behaviour at that level (see Table 5.1).

Table 5.1 Kohlberg's levels of moral reasoning

Level	Stage	Explanation for moral/immoral behaviour
Level 1 Pre-conventional morality	Stage 1 Punishment and obedience orientation	Rules will be obeyed to avoid punishment but if you think you can get away with it then you might break the rules.
	Stage 2 Self-interest orientation	Rules will be followed if it's in your best interest but if there is more to gain from crime, then that becomes more likely.
Level 2 Conventional morality	Stage 3 Good girl/boy orientation	The need for social approval is all important, so less likely to commit crime if those around you would disapprove.
	Stage 4 Law and order orientation	Laws are generally accepted as being right as they help to maintain order, so crime becomes less likely.
Level 3 Post-conventional morality	Stage 5 Social contract orientation	Recognition that the law is part of a social contract that can be changed depending on circumstances. The law isn't always right and so can be broken if it doesn't make sense.
	Stage 6 Ethical principles orientation	Some ethical principles are above the law, particularly if they are part of strongly held personal moral values or beliefs. The law isn't always just and so can be broken if it leads to injustice.

Think!

Which level of moral reasoning is most likely to lead to criminal behaviour?

Which level is least likely to lead to criminal behaviour?

Should law breakers at Level 3 be regarded as criminals?

Studying moral development

Piaget and Kohlberg both used stories about certain situations involving moral issues, which would be read through and followed with questions about what would be the right/wrong thing to do in this situation. Kohlberg's stories were of moral dilemmas and the most famous of these is the Heinz dilemma (see Table 5.2).

Table 5.2 The Heinz dilemma

Heinz's wife was dying from a particular type of cancer. Doctors said a new drug might save her. The drug had been discovered by a local chemist and Heinz tried desperately to buy some of the drug, but the chemist was charging ten times the money it cost to make the drug and this was much more than Heinz could afford. Heinz could only raise half the money, even after help from family and friends. He explained to the chemist that his wife was dying and asked if he could have the drug at a cheaper price or pay the rest of the money later. The chemist refused, saying that he had discovered the drug and was going to make money from it. The husband was desperate to save his wife, so later that night he broke into the chemist and stole the drug.

Questions asked by Kohlberg

1. Should Heinz have stolen the drug?
2. Would it change anything if Heinz did not love his wife?
3. What if the person dying was a stranger, would it make any difference?
4. Should the police arrest the chemist for murder if the woman died?

Kohlberg (1968) used this approach in a longitudinal study of a group of 75 boys over a period of 12 years who were aged between 10 and 16 at the start of the study. Kohlberg found that people move through each of the stages in order from the lower levels through to the higher ones as they get older, although not everyone reached the higher stage and it was unclear whether the two stages at Level 3 were completely separate.

Question time

How did Kohlberg measure a person's level of moral reasoning?

Was this a good way of measuring the level? Why/not?

Were there any problems with Kohlberg's (1968) study? If so, what?

What are cognitive distortions?

The idea of **faulty information processing** can lead to the idea that we make sense of what is coming into our minds in an inappropriate or biased way. Research has linked this faulty information processing with the way criminals interpret other people's behaviour and justify their own actions.

Two examples of cognitive distortions are:

1. Hostile attribution bias.
2. Minimalisation.

Hostile attribution bias

Ever heard the phrase 'what are you looking at' used by anyone? If you have, it's likely that the person saying it was using a hostile attribution bias, as they were assuming that the person looking at them was doing do so in a hostile or negative manner, when in fact they might have been looking at them in an admiring or positive manner.

Hostile attributions occur when an individual misinterprets the behaviour of others and attributes (explains the reasons behind) it to some negative or hostile intention, which was probably not there and this may cause the individual to behave in a hostile or aggressive manner in return.

These **cognitive biases** are probably formed in childhood and, according to Dodge (1980), are linked to **schemas** developed from the experience of being popular or being rejected by their peers. These experiences are likely to have given these children a negative outlook (if rejected) towards their dealings with others and may have been part of a cycle of receiving negative or hostile treatment from others leading to them developing a tendency to respond in this way when faced with future interactions, particularly when the intentions of others were ambiguous.

Minimalisation

This is an attempt to rationalise behaviour by playing down its seriousness or failing to take responsibility for it. A criminal might try to minimise the importance of what they've done because they don't want to accept the guilt that goes with it and because if they did so it would make them feel bad about themselves. Examples of this come from Bandura (1999) who explained how 'euphemistic labelling' is used to make things not sound as bad as they really are, so a rapist might say that 'she was asking for it'. Criminals might also try to disregard or distort the consequences of their behaviour, so a burglar might claim that 'their insurance will cover it'. All these behaviours serve to protect the offender from the harm that might come from having to accept that they have done something wrong or that they have truly hurt someone, this kind of distortion is believed to be particularly common among sex offenders (Langton et al. 2008).

Think!

Have you ever heard these kind of cognitive distortions being used?

What did you think of them at the time? Did they sound credible or ridiculous?

Can you think of any other examples of them being used?

Mini plenary

Match each term to the correct definition by drawing a line to connect them:

Term	Definition
Hostile attribution bias	A view of morality based on the consequences of your actions, e.g. if you get punished then it's bad.
Post-conventional morality	A view of morality based on the belief that the law is right, so if your behaviour breaks the law then it's wrong.
Pre-conventional morality	A cognitive distortion, which makes you think that other people are being hostile to you causing you to be aggressive back.
Minimalisation	A view of morality based on an individual view of morality that says you can break the law if it is unfair or unjust.
Conventional morality	A cognitive distortion, which helps to shift the blame for crime by playing down the importance of it.

AO2 (Application of knowledge): How does this apply in practice?

Interleave me now

Gender bias

Gender bias is one issue in psychological research that seems to occur again and again with the differences between men and women being ignored or sometimes overplayed so much that it can be used an excuse not to bother studying both because they are so different. Of course, all too often, this means not studying women.

Forms of gender bias

Androcentrism is the tendency to focus attention on males at the expense of females.

Alpha bias is one that tends to overplay the importance of gender in our understanding of human behaviour and suggests that men and women are completely different and either implicitly or sometimes explicitly suggests that the behaviour of the two should be explained quite differently.

Beta bias is one that tends to downplay the importance of gender in our understanding of human behaviour and tends to suggest that we can ignore the issue of gender as men and women are basically the same.

Gender bias and moral development

There is a tendency in the study of crime and moral development to ignore the role of women as crime is regarded as a mostly male phenomenon and therefore, why do we need to study women at all?

Carol Gilligan (1982) has criticised Kohlberg on this point as his theory is based primarily on his work with boys and therefore could be argued to have provided an androcentric view of moral development and crime. In addition, she argues that he has also ignored the differences between males and females, as he argues that girls are stuck at the conventional level of morality because they cannot get past the need to maintain relationships and the welfare of family and friends. Boys, on the other hand, are able to deal with more abstract concepts such as justice and fairness and therefore he seems to suggest that boys are morally superior.

Gilligan argues that Kohlberg is ignoring or at least downplaying the value of the ethical concerns of caring for others while at the same time overemphasising the concept of justice. It isn't that women aren't capable of understanding this concept, it's just that they have a different view of the importance of such concepts. Kohlberg's theory regards concepts such as justice as more important, possibly because he is male; therefore, he believes everyone else should.

Gilligan quotes the example of an 11-year-old girl called Amy and her response to the Heinz dilemma, which is not simply to allow the husband to strike out on his own and find the solution but for the husband and wife to work together to find a solution that will be mutually beneficial. For Kohlberg this might indicate a lower level of reasoning but for Gilligan this was the most appropriate answer from someone who values the importance of communication and working together (like Amy!).

Think!

Are concerns over justice more important than the welfare of those you are close to?

Who is right, Gilligan or Kohlberg?

Interleave me now

Cultural bias

Many of the studies conducted into levels of moral reasoning are based in western culture with participants being drawn from America or Europe. This creates a problem as it is difficult to draw conclusions about moral reasoning, even if the same western researchers conduct studies outside of their own country, e.g. Kohlberg did do research in other countries, such as Taiwan, Canada, Mexico and Turkey.

Etic and emic approaches

The idea of imposed etic suggests that standards of behaviour from one culture are being applied to people from another culture. This usually takes the form of applying a standard of behaviour that has been created in one part of the world, e.g. Kohlberg's research into levels of moral reasoning in America, and applying it to people from another part of the world, e.g. levels of moral reasoning in Taiwan.

An emic approach is much more open and suggests that it is only possible to understand the behaviour of other cultures from within that culture, using ideas and concepts that have been taken from that particular culture, rather than another one. In this sense, research would need to do more than simply study people from other cultures but would need to have a deeper understanding of the culture that is being studied and be able to see things from that culture's point of view.

Cultural factors in moral development

Using an emic approach, Jaafar et al. (2004) set out to test the difference between American and Malay adolescents in terms of Kohlberg's levels of moral reasoning. They used one of Kolhberg's moral dilemmas (Joe) to test 134 adolescents, 67 males and 67 females, divided roughly equally between USA and Malaysia. They found that the average level of moral reasoning in America was at Stage 2 with the average level in Malaysia at Stage 3. They attributed most of the difference to the fact that Americans are more concerned with individual rewards and material goods, whereas Malaysians had a strong focus on community and the needs of others and that their morals were largely related to the teachings of the **Qur'an**, which might explain their higher level.

These findings are very different from those of Kohlberg and suggest that the levels of moral reasoning aren't entirely universal and may differ depending on cultural factors and even religion.

Question time

What does gender and culture bias tell us about the study of moral reasoning?

Is it possible to take a truly emic approach to studying other cultures? If so, how?

What does the Jaafar study tell us about levels of moral reasoning?

Seth has been accused of burglary and upon being questioned by the police explained that he hadn't done anything wrong because he needed to feed his family and what else could he do. Harry is also being questioned by the police and is explaining how he came to get into a fight with his neighbour. He explains how every day when he got home from work and closed the door of his car, his neighbour would look at him aggressively from his kitchen window. He had to do something about it!

Explain the responses given by Seth and Harry with reference to the use of cognitive distortions for explaining criminal behaviour?

_____

_____

_____

_____

_____

_____

_____

_____

AO3 (Analysis and evaluation of knowledge): How useful are these explanations for crime?

Evidence for Kohlberg's levels of moral reasoning

Kohlberg himself provided some evidence of his levels of moral reasoning with his longitudinal study that showed the development of moral reasoning of a group of boys through 12 years of their life. This provides evidence of the movement through his stages and the notion that different levels of moral reasoning are associated with responses to moral dilemmas. However, this study did not show a connection to actual criminals as it was a study of non-criminals.

A more comprehensive study of the relationship between moral reasoning and offenders was conducted by Stams et al. (2006) who conducted a meta-analysis of 50 studies looking into the levels of moral reasoning of over 2,000 young offenders, matched for socioeconomic status, gender, cultural background and educational level with a group of over 2,000 young non-offenders. The analysis generally included studies that had used scenarios similar to those used by Kohlberg to be able to compare more directly with Kohlberg's levels.

This comprehensive study revealed a significant difference between the two groups, such that the offender group were operating at a much lower level of moral reasoning and this was particularly true of the older adolescents (above the age of 15), male offenders, those of low intelligence and those that were incarcerated.

However, the authors did recognise that it was only possible for them to show a relationship and that there was no clear causal link. The fact that it was such a large study and that they had found such a highly significant difference did though indicate the strength of the study.

Is morality linked to intelligence?

Kohlberg seems to be arguing in his theory of moral reasoning that the understanding of what is right and wrong and morality are linked to a general level of intelligence, as some people are not capable of the sophisticated understanding of morality that is required at the higher levels. This would seem to stem from a low level of IQ throughout the life of an individual but should be recognisable in early childhood.

However, research by Beißert and Hasselhorn (2016) suggests that morality and intelligence may not be related at all. They recruited 109 primary age children, roughly evenly divided into those that attended regular primary schools and those that attended enrichment programmes for gifted children. The children were given an IQ assessment to determine their level of intelligence and all were tested using a storyboard set of scenarios to determine their level of moral reasoning.

The researchers found that there was no correlation between the intelligence level of the children and their level of moral reasoning, which seems to suggest that Kohlberg was wrong to assume that there might be and that moral reasoning and cognitive ability are completely separate.

However, the researchers do recognise that the children weren't especially young and it might be more useful to conduct similar tests with younger children as this may show more of a correlation. They also admitted, that in order to do the test at all, the children needed to have a certain level of intelligence to answer the questions. Therefore, it might have been more conclusive if they had used children of an even lower level of intelligence to compare to.

Do cognitive distortions explain why people commit crime?

Cognitive distortions are put forward here as an explanation for crime and therefore, it is believed, that people will engage in this kind of thinking before they decide to become involved in crime. However, it could be that these cognitive distortions are nothing more than excuses that people use after their crime to try to explain to themselves and others why they did what they did.

Maruna and Mann (2006) have argued that making excuses is a normal part of life when we have done something wrong and that it is also normal to look for excuses that take the blame away from something that is very close to ourselves and point instead to something that is well removed from us.

According to Maruna and Mann, this is normal and it therefore shouldn't be surprising to find that people involved in crime attempt to do the same thing, particularly when they have done something that is really bad or that most people would find disturbing.

Maruna and Mann suggest that it's not surprising that most research has found that people do this but what they do find surprising is that it has been used to try to explain the causes of offending rather than seeing it as doing the opposite, i.e. doing the crime leads to feeling the need to make the excuse.

According to Maruna and Mann, this is an example of a fundamental attribution error in which the causes are attributed to individual cognitive factors when they should be focused more heavily on social factors that are more likely to be the cause and may also be the reason why some people are more likely to engage in excuse-making than others.

Finally, they make the point that it may seem reasonable to want to make offenders take full responsibility for their actions and not make excuses but, according to Maruna and Mann, this may actually make them more likely to re-offend, rather than less, as if they do take full responsibility it may lead them to the conclusion that they are just that sort of a person and therefore do it again. Whereas, if they can excuse it in some way, they could say that it's not them, it's just their situation at the time or the fact that they were drunk, and so be able to move on and never do it again.

Consequently, trying to avoid offenders using cognitive distortions or excuses for their crimes may not only be incorrect but it may also lead to greater recidivism.

> **Think!**
>
> What does this tell us about the current system of justice, which focuses on the need for criminals to show remorse by admitting their crime?
>
> Should we change the way we reward those who plead guilty?

Evidence for the link between cognitive distortions and crime

The use of cognitive distortions seems to make sense for those involved in certain forms of crime, particularly those where on the face of it, any rational person would find it difficult to understand the thoughts of those involved, e.g. sex offenders.

Blumenthal et al. (1999) set out to study the use of cognitive distortions such as minimalisation and attribution bias in the reasoning of two types of sexual offenders, those that commit adult sexual offences (ASO) and those that commit child sexual offences (CSO). They studied 36 males from the ASO category and 30 males from the CSO category using a range of self-report measures including the Gudjonsson Blame Attribution Inventory (BAI) and a self-deception questionnaire (SDQ) in an attempt to find out how each group made sense of their behaviour.

They found that the ASO group tended to use more external blame attributions for their offences suggesting that the woman had done something to deserve it whereas the CSO group tended to make use of minimalisation, such as sex can make children feel closer to adults.

Both of these findings seem to support the use of cognitive distortions in crime, particularly with the use of minimalisation as even the attribution bias related to adult sexual offences fits with some of the predictions made by this distortion.

The application of cognitive distortions to treatment and therapy

The idea of cognitive distortions has been shown to apply well to certain forms of crime, particularly violent and sexual crime and these are areas that might benefit from treatment programmes that focus on changing an individual's perception of their crime through the use of cognitive behaviour therapy (CBT) and in particular, anger management.

Anger management seems to fit perfectly with the idea of hostile attribution bias as offenders are getting themselves into situations where an aggressive response becomes increasingly likely as they are responding inappropriately to the cues that are being given off by others. In a typical anger management programme, the first stage is cognitive preparation, in which the offender learns to identify the triggers for their anger and then work towards coming up with different interpretations of these situations so that they don't resort to anger and violence.

However, some have argued that such programmes don't work well for certain types of crimes and this has been particularly argued against in the case of non-violent crime whereby the use of anger management can play no part and even in the case of crimes that do involve violence, it has been argued that many of these crimes are premeditated and unrelated to the current state of the perpetrator.

One area where this is increasingly being shown is in the area of domestic violence where anger management is sometimes offered to those who don't have an anger problem and for whom attending an anger management session can be a lot easier than attending an intimate partner violence intervention programme (Jo, 2012).

This suggests that while CBT programmes, such as anger management, seem a perfect fit for dealing with the problems caused by cognitive distortions, they are limited in their application and usefulness, particularly when it comes to non-violent crimes but also in those cases where the violence isn't about anger but is about control, as in the case of domestic violence.

Mini plenary

Using the evaluation points above, try to complete the following table:

Theory	Evidence/arguments for	Evidence/arguments against
Kohlberg's theory		
Cognitive distortions		

A modern issue: can we use cognitive explanations for all forms of crime?

69

AO3 (ANALYSIS AND EVALUATION OF KNOWLEDGE)

Cognitive explanations for crime have the potential or practical applications in the use of cognitive treatments like anger management. However, there is a question mark over whether they should be used for all forms of crime or whether they are only useful for crimes that are based on anger or frustration.

New research

Kathryn Maietta (8 August 2014). Domestic abuse is not an anger management problem, Bangor Daily News *(Special to the BDN).*

In the article, Maietta looks at the problem of how crimes like rape and domestic abuse are the only crimes where questions are asked about the behaviour of the victim, e.g. what did she do to provoke the attack? She argues that far from being a crime wherein the offender loses control, domestic violence is all about control and the offender's attempt to use and maintain it.

The article argues that the idea that domestic abusers have an anger management problem is a myth and that instead their behaviour is premeditated and their frustration only occurs when their victim tries to exert any control. This can be seen quite clearly because the abuser doesn't go around attacking anyone, just their intimate partner, and to everyone else they can seem perfectly normal with no tendency to become angry at all.

However, she argues that abusers are happy to attend anger management sessions because there is less stigma attached to them and often they aren't required to pay for them, whereas they might be required to pay for a batterer's intervention programme.

Finally, she makes the point that until we stop treating domestic abuse as an anger management problem, nothing will be done about it and we will continue to have many more domestic tragedies.

Question time

What does this article tell us about the treatment of criminals?

Should we use anger management for all forms of crime?

What are the problems associated with using anger management for cases of domestic violence?

1. What is the cognitive explanation for offending based on?
2. What is Kohlberg's view of moral development?
3. What are Kohlberg's levels of moral reasoning?
4. How did Kohlberg study moral reasoning?
5. What are cognitive distortions?
6. What is the hostile attribution bias?
7. What is minimalisation?
8. What are the different forms of gender bias in psychology?
9. How does gender bias relate to moral development and crime?
10. What are the different forms of cultural bias in psychology?
11. How does cultural bias relate to moral development and crime?
12. What is the evidence for the link between cognitive distortions and crime?
13. How can cognitive distortions be applied to the treatment of crime?
14. What is the evidence for the relationship between Kohlberg's levels of moral reasoning and crime?
15. Is intelligence linked to crime?
16. Do cognitive distortions explain why people commit crime?

Glossary

Key word	Definition
Cognitive behaviour therapy (CBT)	A talking therapy that can help you manage your problems by changing the way you think and behave.
Cognitive biases	Errors in the way people think that affect the decisions they make.
Cultural bias	The tendency to treat one group more favourably than another based on their culture.
Faulty information processing	Ways of thinking that are in some way biased or distorted.
Fundamental attribution error	The tendency to downplay situational factors in favour of dispositional factors when deciding what is the cause of some behaviour.
Gender bias	Misrepresenting the experiences of men or women, such that the one is regarded more favourably than the other.

Key word	Definition
Gudjonsson blame attribution inventory (BAI)	A self-reported measure of an individual's blame attribution. Blame attribution refers to the process of attempting to construct causal explanations for behaviours displayed by themselves and others.
Intimate partner violence intervention programme	A therapeutic programme designed to prevent those who have committed domestic violence offending again.
Meta-analysis	A method of research using data from a number of previous studies to try to establish an overall trend.
Qur'an	The holy book of Islam.
Recidivism	The tendency of a convicted criminal to re-offend.
Schemas	Mental representations of some aspect of our world; they are packets of related ideas that we develop through experience.
Self-deception questionnaire (SDQ)	A self-reported measure of the extent to which people are deceiving themselves about their true intentions or motivations.

Plenary: Exam style questions and answers with advisory comments

Question 1.

Using an example, explain what is meant by cognitive distortions in relation to offending behaviour. [3 marks]

Marks for this question: AO1 = 3

Advice: In a question like this, it's important to make sure you are clearly explaining the term in relation to offending behaviour, so your example must relate to some form of criminal activity. There is no need to provide any analysis or evaluation as all of the marks are for AO1: Knowledge and understanding.

Possible answer: Cognitive distortions occur due to faulty thinking or faulty information processing. This could be through minimising the importance of your criminal behaviour, e.g. suggesting that you need to make a living to justify your burglary. They can also be in the form of a hostile attribution bias whereby you label other people's behaviour as negative and hostile even though it may not be, e.g. thinking that someone is looking at you in a hostile way when they might not be, which leads to you violently attacking them, when in fact they could have been looking at you in a friendly or admiring way.

Question 2.

Jack, Jim and Jan are discussing the reasons that some people commit crime and others don't. Jack says that some people commit crime just because they think that they can get away with it and that some people have realised that the punishment for crime isn't that bad in comparison to the potential rewards.

Jim agrees but says that most people don't commit crime because they feel the social approval that comes from doing the right thing is more important than the rewards of crime. He also says that some people just respect the law and realise that it is in their best interests to maintain social order.

Jan agrees but argues that some, basically good people, do go against the law if they feel that something needs to be changed, or because it goes against what they feel to be right or they have a good cause.

With reference to the views of Jack, Jim and Jan in the scenario, discuss the levels of moral reasoning and cognitive explanation for offending behaviour. **[16 marks]**

Marks for this question: AO1 = 6, AO2 = 4 and AO3 = 6

Advice: This question is looking for all three skills of: knowledge and understanding; application of knowledge; and analysis and evaluation. As there are 6 marks for AO1 and 6 for AO3, there should be a roughly equal emphasis on knowledge and understanding and evaluation. However, with 4 marks for AO2 on this question, there is also the need for significant reference to the material in the stem. It's important to ensure that you have shown the examiner that you have applied your knowledge to the stem, so it's always a good idea to use some of the words/sentences/phrases from the stem.

Possible answer: Kohlberg uses a stage approach to the understanding of moral development by arguing that moral reasoning develops in levels, with each level having a slightly different understanding of what is right and wrong. The higher the level, the more mature and sophisticated our understanding of right and wrong becomes. Kohlberg wasn't suggesting that these levels would fit with a particular age but that they would fit with different levels of sophistication in the thinking of an individual. Therefore, it may be that younger children are more likely to be at the lower levels but it could be that older children and adults could also be at this level, which might explain their involvement with crime. Each level has two sub-stages, which have an orientation or particular focus on certain principles that drive behaviour at that level.

The first level is the pre-conventional level, which explains that people obey laws and show moral behaviour to avoid punishment and get rewards or because they believe it is in their best interests to follow the rules. This relates to the comments made by Jack, because he is suggesting that people might commit a crime if they think they can get away with it – which fits with the first stage of the pre-conventional level – or because they think that the rewards of crime outweigh the possible punishments – which fits with the second stage of the pre-conventional level.

The second level is the conventional level of morality in which people obey the law because they feel that they want to be seen to be good at the first stage or because they want to maintain the social order at the second stage of this level. The first stage of this level fits with the comments made by Jim when he says the social approval that comes from doing the right thing is more important than the rewards of crime. The second stage of this level fits with Jim when he says that some people just respect the law and realise that it is in their best interests to maintain social order.

The third level is the post-conventional level of morality, which is related to a social contract being made between the people and the law and people will follow the rules as long as the law makes sense in the first stage of this level and as long as the law doesn't go against their own or universal principles of what's right in the second stage of this level. This relates to the comments made by Jan when he says that some, basically good people, do go against the law if they feel that something needs to be changed, or because it goes against what they feel to be right or they have a good cause.

Kohlberg used moral dilemmas with people of different stages to find out what level of moral reasoning they were using, e.g. he conducted a longitudinal study of a group of 75 boys over a period of 12 years who were aged between 10 and 16 at the start of the study. Kohlberg found that people move through each of the stages in order from the lower levels through to the higher ones as they got older, although not everyone reached the higher stage and it was unclear whether the two stages at level 3 were completely separate. However, this study did not show a connection to actual criminals as it was a study of non-criminals.

A more comprehensive study of the relationship between moral reasoning and offenders was conducted by Stams et al who conducted a meta-analysis of 50 studies looking into the levels of moral reasoning of over 2,000 young offenders matched for socioeconomic status, gender, cultural background and educational level with a group of over 2,000 young non-offenders. The analysis generally included studies that had used scenarios similar to that used by Kohlberg in order to be able to compare more directly with Kohlberg's levels.

This comprehensive study revealed a significant difference between the two groups, such that the offender group were operating at a much lower level of moral reasoning and this was particularly true of the older adolescents (above the age of 15), male offenders, those of low intelligence and those that were incarcerated.

However, it was only possible for them to show a relationship and that there was no clear causal link. The fact that it was such a large study and they had found such a highly significant difference did though indicate the strength of the study.

Furthermore, Kohlberg has been accused of both gender bias and cultural bias in his research. Carol Gilligan has criticised Kohlberg for being gender biased, as his theory is based primarily on his work with boys and therefore could be argued to have provided an androcentric view of moral development and crime.

Kohlberg could be accused of using an imposed etic by applying the standards of behaviour from one culture to another culture, e.g. Kohlberg's research into levels of moral reasoning in America, and then applying it to people from another part of the world, e.g. levels of moral reasoning in Taiwan.

References

Bandura, A. (1999). Moral disengagement in the perpetration of inhumanities. *Personality and Social Psychology Review*. [Special Issue on Evil and Violence], 3: 193–209.

Beißert, H.M. and Hasselhorn, M. (2016). Individual differences in moral development: Does intelligence really affect children's moral reasoning and moral emotions? *Frontiers in Psychology*, 7: 1961.

Blumenthal, S., Gudjonsson, G. and Burns, J. (1999). Cognitive distortions and blame attribution in sex offenders against adults and children. *Child Abuse & Neglect*, 23(2): 129143.

Dodge, K.A. (1980). Social cognition and children's aggressive behavior. *Child development*, 51(1): 162–170.

Gilligan, C. (1982). *In a Different Voice: Psychological Theory and Women's Development*. Cambridge, Massachusetts: Harvard University Press.

Jaafar, J., Kolodinsky, P., McCarthy, S. and Schroder, V. (2004). The impact of cultural norms and values on the moral judgement of Malay and American adolescents: A brief report. In B.N. Setiadi, A. Supratiknya, W., J. Lonner and Y. H., Poortinga (eds.), *Ongoing themes in psychology and culture*: Proceedings from the 16th International Congress of the International Association for Cross-Cultural Psychology.

Jo, K. (5 January 2012). Anger management classes likely to increase domestic abuse, *HealthyPlace*. Retrieved on 19 February 2020 from www.healthyplace.com/blogs/verbalabuseinrelationships/2012/01/anger-management-likely-to-increase-domestic-abuse.

Kohlberg, L. (1968). The child as a moral philosopher. *Psychology Today* 2(4): 25–30.

Langton, C.M., Barbaree, H.E., Harkins, L., Arenovich, T., McNamee, J., Peacock, E.J., Dalton, A., Hansen, K.T. et al. (2008). Denial and minimization among sexual offenders: Posttreatment presentation and association with sexual recidivism. *Criminal Justice and Behavior*, 35(1): 69–98.

Maietta, K. (8 August 2014). Domestic abuse is not an anger management problem. *Bangor Daily News*.

Maruna, S. and Mann, R.E. (2006). A fundamental attribution error? Rethinking cognitive distortions. *Legal and Criminological Psychology*, 11(2): 155–177.

Stams, G.J., Brugman, D., Deković, M., Van Rosmalen, L., Van Der Laan, P. and Gibbs, J.C. (2006). The moral judgment of juvenile delinquents: A meta-analysis. *Journal of Abnormal Child Psychology*, 34(5): 692–708.

Chapter 6
Psychological explanations of offending behaviour 3 – Psychodynamic explanations

Spec check

Psychological explanations of offending behaviour 3 – psychodynamic explanations.

AO1 (Knowledge and understanding): Psychological explanations of offending behaviour 3 – psychodynamic explanations

The psychodynamic explanation of offending

The origins of psychodynamic explanations come from the work of Sigmund Freud who provided an explanation for personality development based on principles related to the dynamic interaction between natural instincts and parental behaviour. This suggests that the first few years of life are particularly important in our development and therefore it is likely that any psychodynamic explanation will focus on what happens in that period in order to understand later criminal tendencies.

Freud himself didn't provide an explanation of offending behaviour but his ideas have been used later to explain this phenomenon, specifically in relation to the development (or lack of it) of the superego. Bowlby, working in a psychodynamic tradition, used his maternal deprivation hypothesis to explain later delinquency.

How do Freudian ideas relate to crime?

The superego is clearly important to a Freudian understanding of morality, as it is what Freud believes gives the child its conscience. Freud argued that the superego is necessary to provide the child with an alternative motivation from the demanding and uncontrolled id, which might push the child towards behaviour that could be seen as immoral and unsatisfactory.

Psychodynamic theory looks at the role of conflicts in the development of future personality and it is believed that these conflicts will motivate future deviant acts. Conflicts during the phallic stage in particular may disrupt the normal development of the superego and consequently the development of the individual's conscience. The idea of an inadequate superego has, therefore, been developed after Freud's death and now forms a very important part of a psychodynamic understanding of what might push an individual towards criminal behaviour.

According to Blackburn (1993), a disturbance in the development of any part of the personality will lead to maladaptive behaviour and in particular an inadequate superego can cause problems with ego control and the ability to delay gratification. There are three forms of the inadequate superego that relate to criminal behaviour:

The harsh superego – arises from an overdeveloped conscience and is characterised by a person that has strong feelings of guilt and instead of dealing with them internally, externalises them by seeking out situations where they can be punished, e.g. by being caught for committing crime.

The weak superego – arises from an underdeveloped conscience and is characterised by a person that has a lack of control over the demands of the id, which pushes them towards uncontrolled, guiltless acts. Such a person may even develop psychopathic tendencies as they were never able to identify with either parent, which leads to narcissistic tendencies, such as a lack of empathy and a desire to exploit others.

The deviant superego – arises from a normal process of superego development by means of identification with the same-sex parent and the adoption of their moral values. Unfortunately, in this case, the parent has deviant values, which are then picked up by the child, encouraging them to engage in criminal behaviour.

Question time

What is the superego?

How do problems with the superego occur?

Why do problems with the superego lead to offending?

How does maternal deprivation relate to crime?

Psychodynamic explanations have a strong focus on the role of the parents during the early years, as their reactions to the conflicts that are normally experienced by the child are key to normal development. Freudian ideas have particularly focused on the role of the father in this process and this fits well with the common sense view that the lack of a father figure can cause problems for the development of a child that has not experienced rules and discipline. However, John Bowlby was much more concerned with the role of the mother in development, particularly during the very early years of a child's development, the so-called critical period from birth to around the age of two and a half to three years old.

In line with psychodynamic theory, Bowlby believed that an adult's personality was heavily influenced by what happened in the early years and in particular the bond between the mother and her infant. For Bowlby (1951), 'what is believed to be essential for mental health is that the infant and young child should experience a warm, intimate and continuous relationship with his mother (or permanent mother substitute)'. In this situation, the child will grow up with the ability to recognise and deal with the demands of anxiety and guilt. However, should the child be deprived of this in some way, through separation from their mother for example, then the child will suffer damaging consequences, which last through to their adult life.

The main long-term consequence relevant to criminality is the development of affectionless psychopathy, which is a personality type characterised by an inability to feel love or guilt and the lack of a conscience, such that these individuals don't care about others and therefore are quite content to commit crimes against them, particularly theft.

In his study of 44 juvenile thieves, Bowlby (1944) was able to compare the background and personality of a group of 44 boys who had been referred to the London Child Guidance Clinic with a history of stealing (although only a minority had ever been charged in court), with a group of 44 boys who had also been referred to the clinic but had no history of stealing (the control group). Interviews with the boys showed that 14 had an affectionless personality and interviews with their families revealed that 12 of the 14 had experienced separation from their mother for 6 months or more during the critical period. Similar interviews with the control group and their families revealed that none of them were affectionless and only two had suffered prolonged separation in the critical period. For Bowlby, this was evidence that prolonged separation during the critical period caused affectionless psychopathy, which would lead those affected into criminal behaviour.

Mini plenary

Complete the following table to show the similarities and differences between Freudian ideas (Blackburn) of the development of crime and Bowlby's view of the development of crime:

	Freudian ideas	Bowlby
Similarities		
Differences		

AO2 (Application of knowledge): How does this apply in practice?

Interleave me now

The psychodynamic approach

The psychodynamic approach is associated with the work of Freud on the structure and development of personality.

The structure of personality

Freud believed that personality is divided into three parts:

Id – is the first part to develop, is present from birth and is linked to survival, as it makes the child demanding. It is based on the **pleasure principle** as it is focused on getting what the child wants and seeks immediate gratification.

Ego – is the next part to develop from around 18 months old and is the rational part of the personality. It is based on the **reality principle** and is focused on satisfying the demands of the Id but in a more reasonable manner as it mediates between the id and the superego.

Superego – is the final part to develop from around three years old and is the moral part of the personality. It is based on the **morality principle** and encourages the child to behave in the right way through the formation of a conscience, which makes the child feel guilt.

The development of personality: Psychosexual stages

Freud believed that personality develops through a series of fixed developmental stages that occur at around the same age in all children. In each stage, the focus is on a different area of the body (**erogenous zone**) and Freud believed that unresolved conflicts at each stage could lead to fixation (becoming stuck) so that the child would be unable to move on to the next stage and further develop their personality.

Table 6.1 Freud's psychosexual stages of development

Stage	Focus	Source of conflict	Fixation
Oral 0–1 year	Stimulation achieved by putting things in the mouth.	Being allowed, or not, to put things into the mouth, e.g. a dummy.	**Oral fixation –** nail-biting, pen-chewing, dependent and sarcastic.
Anal 1–3 years	Stimulation achieved by holding in and expelling faeces from the anus.	Toilet training with both the child and the parent trying to take control.	**Anal retentive –** obsessively tidy and organised, and mean. **Anal expulsive –** messy and overgenerous.

Table 6.1 continued

Stage	Focus	Source of conflict	Fixation
Phallic 3–5 years	Stimulation is achieved through the genitals.	Oedipus or Electra complex in which the child will have strong feelings of desire for the same-sex parent and hatred of the opposite-sex parent.	**Phallic** – failure to identify with the same-sex parent can lead to selfish and uncontrolled behaviour.

As each of these stages is tied into the development of the three parts of the personality, it is easy to see that failure to identify at the phallic stage can lead to a disruption in the development of the superego. This has been shown (see p. 76) to potentially lead to criminal behaviour, so the phallic stage is particularly important. Freud believed that the father was particularly important for the development of a boy's moral code as they experienced **castration anxiety**, which would provide a strong motivation to take on the morals of their father. Bowlby believed that the father would play '**second fiddle**' to the mother in the development of personality as only maternal deprivation would cause the development of an affectionless character.

Question time

What are the three parts of the personality and what principles are they based on?

What kinds of conflicts are related to the development of the personality?

How do these conflicts lead an individual into immoral or criminal behaviour?

Interleave me now

Free will and determinism

The question of whether our behaviour is determined by factors that are beyond our control or whether we are able to exert complete control using our free will is extremely important in the whole of psychology but is particularly important in the study of criminal behaviour. Do we accept that criminal behaviour is determined by forces that mean some people are bound to behave in a criminal manner? This is crucially important in terms of how we decide to deal with offending behaviour: if people have no control then can we really say that they are responsible for their behaviour?

Types of determinism

Biological determinism

A view that follows on directly from the assumptions of the biological approach to human behaviour and argues that all behaviour is in the first instance driven by biological factors (genes, hormones, nervous system, etc.) If we attempt to explain any form of human behaviour we must at some point come back to the view that our responses are triggered by neural signals in our brain leading to messages being sent to our muscles telling us to behave in some way. All of this is ultimately governed by our **genetic make-up** and therefore biology can explain all forms of human behaviour. Alongside this, we could argue that all behaviour is adaptive and therefore governed by evolutionary factors.

Environmental determinism

This view follows on from the behaviourist approach and the belief that all behaviour is the result of some form of **conditioning**. Skinner regarded free will as an 'illusion' and suggested that most, if not all behaviour is driven by its consequences. We have learned through positive and negative reinforcement that behaviour has consequences and therefore we don't make decisions, we merely follow the path that has been set out for us to follow by parents, teachers, bosses, etc.

Psychic determinism

This view follows on from the psychodynamic approach and the belief that all behaviour is driven by our unconscious mind. Freud saw behaviour resulting from innate instincts that lead us into childhood conflicts. These conflicts are repressed into our unconscious mind and push our behaviour in certain directions, generally to avoid anxiety or to satisfy the demands of different parts of our personality. The behaviour that results from this is not under our conscious control but merely the ego's response to anxiety causing dilemmas.

This last type of determinism is particularly relevant to psychodynamic explanations of offending behaviour as it would help to explain the influence of an inadequate superego on our behaviour but it is also relevant to Bowlby's theory. Bowlby believed that the **unconscious conflicts** that arise from maternal deprivation would represent themselves in feelings of anxiety, depression and revenge, which would influence the child throughout their life. In this situation, it would seem that individuals experiencing these effects wouldn't be able to stop themselves from behaving in destructive and even criminal ways.

Think!

Could it be that factors beyond someone's control push them into offending?

Is free will an 'illusion' or do people make a conscious decision to commit crime or not?

If it is free will, what makes some people commit crime and others not?

Over 70 per cent of women with dependent children now go out to work, which is higher than the number of women and men in work without dependent children, although it is still lower than the number of men with dependent children who work, which is currently over 90 per cent.

Explain one psychodynamic explanation for offending with reference to the statistics above.

_____

_____

_____

_____

_____

_____

_____

_____

AO3 (Analysis and evaluation of knowledge): How useful are these explanations for crime?

Methodological issues

The main methods employed in researching psychodynamic explanations are case studies and interviews. Freud himself used case studies that were based on interviews with his patients to discover the unconscious motivations for their behaviour. Bowlby used interviews with 88 boys and their families in his study of 44 juvenile thieves.

There are a few strengths and weaknesses involved in the use of interviews in psychological research:

On the positive side, interviews do have the ability to delve more deeply into issues so that things like unconscious motivations might be uncovered, which wouldn't be possible with other methods that only scratch the surface. This level of depth may raise the validity of the research as you are more able to find out the true causes of behaviour. This is particularly the case when dealing with sensitive issues of the sort being discussed here.

On the negative side, there is the possibility of interviewer bias in which the person doing the interviewing may structure or ask the questions in such a way that it is clear what kind of response is required. This is particularly true when the person doing the interviews is aware of the desired outcome or hypothesis (both Bowlby and Freud carried out the interviews).

Furthermore, there is the possibility of social desirability bias in which the person being interviewed may answer the questions in a way that might be seen to be more appropriate and not make them look bad. It could be that people being interviewed about their criminal behaviour might be keen to find an excuse by blaming factors beyond their control.

Trying to find the motives behind criminal behaviour is an incredibly difficult thing to do and while it may seem useful to try to get to the heart of the problem by finding out in detail the motives that drive the behaviour with the use of interviews, you run the risk of only finding out what the interviewee wants to tell you, or even worse what you were hoping to find because you made the interview go in that direction.

Alternative explanations

As stated earlier (see p. 80), there is an issue with working on the basis that all behaviour is determined by factors beyond the control of the individual, but even if you do accept that behaviour is determined, then there are other factors that could determine your behaviour.

Biological determinism argues that behaviour is controlled by biological processes such as genes and neural mechanisms. As discussed in Chapter 3, these factors may play a part as it could be that a person has low activity in their MAOA gene, which could push them towards aggressive behaviour or low levels of activity in their prefrontal cortex, which might predispose them to similar acts of violence or even both!

Environmental determinism would suggest that learning and the experiences that have been encountered through life would be important, such that an individual who has been around those who are criminal may have picked up the values and techniques associated with crime, as explained in differential association theory.

However, a better approach than all these alternatives might be take a soft deterministic approach in which there is an acceptance that all of these factors might play a part but at the same time recognising that even when faced with all these pressures, we still have a choice about which path to choose. This would at least offer the possibility that free will plays some part and help to explain why it is that those individuals who may have had similar experiences to criminals, or even have a similar genetic make-up, choose a different path and don't commit crime.

> **Think!**
>
> Do these alternative explanations provide a better explanation than the psychodynamic ones?
>
> Why might soft determinism be better?

Gender bias

The focus on male development in psychodynamic theory is evident throughout the work of Freud and Bowlby. Bowlby only interviewed boys as part of his study into affectionless psychopathy and in his discussion of the importance of maternal care and its influence on mental health, he constantly refers to how this will affect *him* and what *his* response will be (although this could just be because he was rather old-fashioned and referred to everyone as 'he' regardless!)

A more significant issue with psychodynamic theory is recognised by Blackburn (1993) in that Freud had argued that males would have a stronger superego than females, as they have a much more powerful motivation in the form of castration anxiety (which clearly isn't experienced by females) and so males would be more moral than females.

This goes against statistical evidence, which clearly shows that males are more likely to be involved in crime than females and even if you were to argue that males might be more likely to be caught and convicted, this still couldn't make up for the overwhelming proportion of males arrested, cautioned or convicted, compared to females. Furthermore, there is evidence from longitudinal studies to suggest that females are more moral than males, particularly in the area of empathetic responses. Mestre et al. (2009) found that females aged 13–16 responded more empathetically to scenarios on a questionnaire than did males, however there are problems with this type of questioning (see pp. 49–50).

It seems that if gender is a significant factor, it is more likely to be in the opposite direction from that suggested by Freud and there doesn't appear to be any compelling reason why boys who were maternally deprived would be more likely to turn to crime than girls, which brings into question the whole basis of psychodynamic explanations.

Is there evidence for psychodynamic explanations?

It is often suggested that Freud's work is based on pseudoscientific assumptions that are both difficult to prove and to disprove, which has led some to argue that his ideas are purely theoretical and therefore have no evidence behind them. Bowlby does provide evidence from his 44 thieves study but we have already mentioned some of the problems with that study and there are further problems arising from the actual conclusions drawn from the statistics, in that only 17 of the juvenile thieves were actually maternally deprived and only 14 of them were affectionless psychopaths. This suggests that it was actually more common for them not to be maternally deprived and not to be affectionless psychopaths.

Further problems with psychodynamic assumptions are noted by Blackburn (1993) who recognises that the findings of research showing the connection between personality conflicts and criminal behaviour are (necessarily) conducted after the crime has been committed and therefore the disturbance may have been caused by the involvement in crime rather than the other way round, so it seems that there is a problem with causation also.

There is always a problem working with unconscious conflicts, which makes psychodynamic theory difficult to test, although it does seem that with the shift towards cognitive explanations in psychology there is more of an acceptance that the mind does have an effect on behaviour and this is now being supported by neurological evidence, which is showing the biological source of some of these mental processes.

Mini plenary

Using the evaluation points above, try to identify arguments for and against psychodynamic explanations for offending behaviour:

Arguments for	Arguments against

A modern issue: can we blame parents for their children's criminal behaviour?

A major issue that arises from psychological research is the extent to which criminal behaviour is just the fault of the individual and their lack of morality or whether it is due to problems in their childhood and therefore the fault of their parents. A particular issue is whether it is the presence of the father or mother that is crucially important in the development of morals in a child.

New research

Let's talk about gang culture's elephant in the room: absent black fathers. The Telegraph News, www.telegraph.co.uk (29 August 2018).

In the article, Sewell talks about his role as a member of the Youth Justice Board and recognising that so many of the young offenders he encountered came from the black community and could easily have been his own sons or grandsons. He wanted to identify the reasons behind this, as Conservative politicians were calling for tougher action and sociologists were blaming austerity.

His conclusion is (after talking to the boys themselves) that they are like Hamlets, haunted by the ghosts of their absent fathers. He reports that the boys themselves say that they are like the lost sons as 'no one knows what to do with us'.

Sewell questions the rise of black feminism in which politicians like Diane Abbott have suggested that women are more than capable of bringing up these boys on their own. The boys themselves question this and describe the father going AWOL as being like a form of post-traumatic stress disorder, leaving them isolated and in danger.

Sewell questions both the overly sympathetic and overly authoritarian approaches as neither is identifying the real cause of the problem. He argues that the answer doesn't lie in more youth clubs or more police on the street but in psychological interventions in which the boys can confront their own demons and start to make a change to their lives.

Question time

What does this article tell us about the causes of crime?

Do you think it is reasonable to suggest that offending is caused by the absent father?

What could the father have done that the mother didn't?

Does this fit with the psychodynamic explanations looked at in this chapter?

Chapter plenary

1. Where do psychodynamic explanations come from?
2. How do Freudian ideas relate to crime?
3. What are the three different types of superego that relate to crime?
4. How does maternal deprivation relate to crime?
5. What evidence does Bowlby use to show this relationship?
6. What is the structure of the personality according to Freud?
7. How does personality develop according to Freud?
8. What are the different types of determinism?
9. How might these lead to crime?
10. What are the methodological issues involved in psychodynamic explanations?
11. What are the alternative explanations for crime?
12. How can psychodynamic explanations be seen as gender biased?
13. Are absent fathers responsible for crime?

Glossary

Key word	Definition
44 juvenile thieves	Bowlby's study of a group of boys who were referred to his clinic and had a history of stealing that he compared to a similar group who had not been stealing.
Ability to defer gratification	Being able to wait to receive pleasure rather than just getting what you want now.
Affectionless psychopathy	A personality that has no emotional connection to anyone and is completely focused on selfish needs.
Castration anxiety	The fear that the male genitalia are going to be removed.
Conditioning	A learning process that involves the use of some form of external influence.

Key word	Definition
Critical period	A period of time in which it is vitally important that certain things happen, e.g. constant mother love in the first three years.
Ego control	The ability to inhibit the expression of basic emotional impulses.
Erogenous zone	An area of the body that is sensitive to stimulation, e.g. pleasure is felt when it is stimulated.
Genetic make-up	The physical make-up of the human body.
Inadequate superego	The idea that the conscience hasn't developed properly.
Interviewer bias	The tendency of an interviewer to push the interviewee towards giving the answers that they want.
Morality principle	Behaviour is motivated by the desire to do what is right and avoid doing what is wrong.
Narcissistic tendencies	Being excessively focused on yourself and having little regard for others.
Pleasure principle	The instinctive drive to receive pleasure and avoid pain.
Reality principle	The ability to hold back the demands of the id and fit in with the demands of the real world.
Second fiddle	Not being the most important thing or person in a certain situation.
Social desirability bias	The tendency to give the kind of answers to questions that you think the questioner wants to hear in order to make yourself look good.
Unconscious conflicts	A serious problem that is hidden in the mind but can still influence our behaviour.
Validity	Being factually sound such that it represents something that is real.

Plenary: Exam-style questions and answers with advisory comments

Question 1.

Outline one psychodynamic explanation of offending behaviour.   [3 marks]

Marks for this question: AO1 = 3

Advice: In a question like this, it's important to make sure you are clearly outlining what is involved in one explanation and how it relates to offending behaviour. One way to do this is to provide a relevant example to help you. Try to make sure that you are only outlining one as to do two would waste time and wouldn't get any extra marks, in fact, it might do the opposite. There is no need to provide any analysis or evaluation as all of the marks are for AO1: Knowledge and understanding.

Possible answer: One psychodynamic explanation for offending behaviour is related to Bowlby's theory of maternal deprivation. Bowlby argues that a child needs a warm, intimate and continuous relationship with their mother in the first three years and should the child be deprived of this in some way, through separation from their mother for example, then the child will suffer damaging consequences, which last through to their adult life. The main long-term consequence relevant to criminality is the development of **affectionless psychopathy**, which is a personality type characterised by an inability to feel love or guilt and the lack of a conscience such that these individuals don't care about others and therefore are quite content to commit crimes against them, particularly theft.

Question 2.

Describe and evaluate one or more psychodynamic explanations of offending behaviour. **[16 marks]**

Marks for this question: AO1 = 6 and AO3 = 10

Advice: This question asks about one or more explanations, which means that you need to make a decision about whether to just focus on one in lots of detail or both in less detail. There will need to be a breadth/depth trade-off as just doing one will require more depth and doing two will require greater breadth.

This question is looking for both skills of knowledge and understanding, and analysis and evaluation. As there are 6 marks for AO1 and 10 for AO3, there should be greater emphasis on the evaluation. However, all such extended writing questions are marked holistically and therefore it is important that the knowledge is accurate and detailed and that the evaluation is clear and effective.

Possible answer: The origins of psychodynamic explanations come from the work of Sigmund Freud who provided an explanation for personality development based on principles related to the dynamic interaction between natural instincts and parental behaviour. This suggests that the first few years of life are particularly important in our development and therefore it is likely that any psychodynamic explanation will focus on what happens in that period in order to understand later criminal tendencies.

Freud himself didn't provide an explanation of offending behaviour but his ideas have been used later to explain this phenomenon, specifically in relation to the development (or lack of it) of the superego.

The superego is clearly important to a Freudian understanding of morality as it is what Freud believes gives the child its conscience. Freud argued that the superego is necessary to provide the child with an alternative motivation from the demanding and uncontrolled id that might push the child towards behaviour that could be seen as immoral and unsatisfactory.

The idea of an inadequate superego has, therefore, been developed after Freud's death and now forms a very important part of a psychodynamic understanding of what might push an individual towards criminal behaviour.

According to Blackburn, a disturbance in the development of any part of the personality will lead to maladaptive behaviour and in particular an inadequate superego can cause problems with ego control and the ability to delay gratification. There are three forms of the inadequate superego that relate to criminal behaviour:

The **harsh superego** – arises from an overdeveloped conscience and is characterised by a person that has strong feelings of guilt and instead of dealing with them internally, externalises them by seeking out situations where they can be punished, e.g. by being caught for committing crime.

The **weak superego** – arises from an underdeveloped conscience and is characterised by a person that has a lack of control over the demands of the id, which pushes them towards uncontrolled, guiltless acts. Such a person may even develop psychopathic tendencies as they were never able to identify with either parent, which leads to narcissistic tendencies, such as a lack of empathy and a desire to exploit others.

The **deviant superego** – arises from a normal process of superego development by means of identification with the same-sex parent and the adoption of their moral values. Unfortunately, in this case, the parent has deviant values, which are then picked up by the child, encouraging them to engage in criminal behaviour.

The focus on male development in psychodynamic theory is evident throughout the work of Freud. Freud argued that males would have a stronger superego than females, as they have a much more powerful motivation in the form of castration anxiety (which clearly isn't experienced by females) and so males would be more moral than females.

This goes against statistical evidence, which clearly shows that males are more likely to be involved in crime than females and even if you were to argue that males might be more likely to be caught and convicted, this still couldn't make up for the overwhelming proportion of males arrested, cautioned or convicted compared to females. Furthermore, there is evidence from longitudinal studies to suggest that females are more moral than males, particularly in the area of empathetic responses. Mestre et al. found that females aged 13–16 responded more empathetically to scenarios on a questionnaire than did males. It seems that if gender is a significant factor then it is more likely to be in the opposite direction from that suggested by Freud.

The use of questionnaires in the Mestre study and the use of interviews by Freud himself can be questioned as there is the possibility of interviewer bias in which the person doing the interviewing may structure or ask the questions in such a way that it is clear what kind of response is required. This is particularly true when the person doing the interviews is aware of the desired outcome or hypothesis.

Furthermore, there is the possibility of social desirability bias in which the person being interviewed may answer the questions in a way that might be seen to be more appropriate and not make them look bad. It could be that people being interviewed about their criminal behaviour might be keen to find an excuse by blaming factors beyond their control.

However, on the positive side, interviews do have the ability to delve more deeply into issues so that things like unconscious motivations might be uncovered, which wouldn't be possible with other methods that only scratch the surface. This level of depth may raise the validity of the research as you are more able to find out the true causes of behaviour. This is particularly the case when dealing with sensitive issues of the sort being discussed here.

This leads on to another issue, which is working on the basis that all behaviour is determined by factors beyond the control of the individual, because even if you do accept that behaviour is determined, then there are other factors that could determine your behaviour.

Biological determinism argues that behaviour is controlled by biological processes such as genes and neural mechanisms. These factors may play a part as it could be that a person has low activity in their MAOA gene, which could push them towards aggressive behaviour or low levels of activity in their prefrontal cortex, which might predispose them to similar acts of violence or even both!

This suggests that there may be alternative explanations that have a lot more scientific evidence behind them than the work of Freud.

References

Blackburn, R. (1993). *The Psychology of Criminal Conduct: Theory, Research and Practice*. West Sussex: John Wiley & Sons.

Bowlby, J. (1944). Forty-four juvenile thieves: their characters and home-life (II). *International Journal of Psycho-Analysis*, 25: 107–128.

Bowlby, J. (1951). *Maternal Care and Mental Health* (Vol. 2). Geneva: World Health Organization.

Mestre, M.V., Samper, P., Frías, M.D. and Tur, A.M. (2009). Are women more empathetic than men? A longitudinal study in adolescence. *The Spanish Journal of Psychology*, 12(1): 76–83.

The Telegraph (2018). Let's talk about gang culture's elephant in the room: absent black fathers. www.telegraph.co.uk (29 August).

Chapter 7
Dealing with offending behaviour 1 – Custodial sentencing and behaviour modification in custody

Spec check

> Dealing with offending behaviour: the aims of custodial sentencing and the psychological effects of custodial sentencing; recidivism; behaviour modification in custody.

AO1 (Knowledge and understanding): Dealing with offending behaviour 1 – custodial sentencing and behaviour modification in custody

What are the aims of custodial sentencing?

Across the world, the most common way of dealing with offenders is to make them spend some time in prison. Custodial sentencing is just that, the process whereby, having been found guilty of a crime, someone is removed from the rest of society by being placed in an institution (prison or young offender's institution).

But why do we do it? There are regularly questions asked about its usefulness, particularly in relation to the high rate of re-offending.

Retribution – Most people would recognise the need for an offender to be punished in some way as most people will have been taught as a child that if you do something wrong then you have to pay for it. Going to prison is one way that offenders can be made to pay for their crime, as the old saying goes 'if you can't do the time then don't do the crime'.

Incapacitation – One of the main aims is to simply remove the offender from society, which in itself serves two purposes: to prevent the offender from committing further crime; to protect the public from potentially dangerous individuals who may pose a threat depending on the nature of their crime, e.g. violent crime.

Deterrence – It is important that offenders aren't allowed to get away with something because if they are, then this might encourage them to do more of the same. This works on behaviourist principles, as if a behaviour is punished then it is less likely to be repeated. They need to be made an example of so that everyone can see the consequences of crime and then others will be put off doing the crime. This is the logic behind public displays of punishment such as public flogging.

Reformation/Rehabilitation – This aims to try to change the offender while they are in prison, so that by the time they come out they are ready to rejoin society and make a useful contribution rather than just going back to their old ways. Reform means to make changes to something and so while in prison, the offender should receive some form of training or treatment that will help them to be returned to normal life, e.g. learning functional skills.

What is the problem of recidivism?

One of the main problems with custodial sentencing is the rate of re-offending, which is known as recidivism and looks at how likely it is that once released from prison, someone will commit another crime and end up back in there.

According to statistics released by the ministry of justice in 2018, 38 per cent of adults released from custodial sentencing will reoffend within 12 months and for sentences of less than 12 months in duration, that figure increases to 64.5 per cent. These figures are quite high and suggest that prison isn't working as a deterrent even if it is fulfilling some of the other aims.

There is a wide range of recidivism rates across the world (see Table 7.1), which is partially due to the way the figures are put together and also partially due to the different approaches taken by each of these countries. In Norway, the focus is very much on rehabilitation as prisoners are taught new skills and live in a nice environment. This is sometimes accused of being a soft option for those imprisoned in Norway but it does seem to work.

Table 7.1 Rates of recidivism in different countries

Country	Recidivism rate
Australia	53%
France	26%
Israel	18%
Netherlands	35%
Norway	20%
South Korea	25%
USA	44%

Adapted from figures published on Wellcome Open Research, 2019; 4: 28. Published by Yukhnenko et al. (2019) online 1 November.

Think!

What do you think most people would say prison should be like? Should it be easy or hard?

Why do you think some people would say it should be hard?

Does that fit with the Norway experience?

What other factors might influence whether someone re-offends or not?

What are the psychological effects of custodial sentencing?

Apart from the problem of recidivism, there are other potentially negative effects, which bring into question the usefulness of putting people into such institutions.

Mental health and suicide – Prison can be very hard to cope with, particularly for those that are new to it and this can cause anxiety and depression. Prisoners are also at increased risk of self-harm and suicide: the Centre for Mental Health has published statistics showing that the number of suicides in prison rose from 89 in 2015 to 119 in 2016 and that in the same period cases of self-harm went up by 26 per cent. This suggests that prisoners are at an increased risk of suicide and self-harm than the general public and this is particularly true for first timers. Figures released by the Prisons and Probation Ombudsman (PPO) state that 10 per cent of the self-inflicted deaths investigated between 2007 and 2013 had taken place during an individual's first three days in custody (PPO 2014).

Institutionalisation – A further problem with imprisonment arises from the fact that spending so much time in a closed environment such as a prison can lead to prisoners becoming so used to it that they find it hard to cope outside. It is important for prison staff that prisoners are controlled, so they will try to create a structure and routine that the prisoners get used to. Everything is provided for prisoners: food, a bed, a sense of belonging and many of these things may be more difficult to obtain outside of prison, all of which might make prison seem quite attractive and lead to further recidivism.

Question time

What is meant by recidivism?

Why might custodial sentencing be linked to mental health problems and even suicide?

Why might some people want to stay in prison?

What is behaviour modification?

In the learning approach, you will have seen how behaviourism explains that all behaviour is learned through the processes of either classical conditioning or operant conditioning. If this is true, then it should also be possible to unlearn behaviour using similar principles. Of particular interest in this section, is the use of operant conditioning principles and in particular the use of reinforcement to change behaviour.

According to the Law of Effect, any behaviour that is followed by pleasant consequences is likely to be repeated and therefore the best way to change behaviour is to try to associate the desired behaviour with something pleasant, which is the basic idea behind behaviour modification. Good behaviour on the part of prisoners will be repeated if it is followed by some kind of reward or privilege.

How does the token economy work?

An example of behaviour modification is the token economy system, which works on the basis of operant conditioning in that desirable behaviour can be exchanged for some form of token, which can in turn be exchanged for some form of privilege. In prison, desirable behaviour is likely to be sticking to the rules, staying out of fights and generally doing what you are told. Privileges are likely to come in the form of time out of your cell, being able to wear your own clothes and even having a TV in your cell.

A system could be introduced whereby points or some other form of token are given each time a desirable behaviour is shown – these will be secondary reinforcers as they have no value in themselves but can be exchanged for something that is more directly reinforcing such as those privileges described above or just nice food!

In the UK, the government operates the Incentives and Earner Privileges scheme (IEP), which works on the principles of a token economy with prisoners starting out at a basic level, which provides few privileges and then moving up to enhanced or even super enhanced, which allows access to longer visiting and the ability to spend more money in the prison on things like cigarettes and sweets, etc. Obviously, it is also possible to be punished for bad behaviour and these privileges will then be taken away.

Mini plenary

Without referring back to the text, provide definitions of the following terms:

Retribution _____

Incapacitation _____

Deterrence _____

Reformation/Rehabilitation _____

Recidivism _____

Institutionalisation _____

AO2 (Application of knowledge): How does this apply in practice?

Interleave me now

The learning approach – behaviourism

The behavioural approach has a number of assumptions about human behaviour but one of the most influential is the view that behaviour is governed by conditioning. Skinner (1953) famously argued that free will is an illusion and believed that it was possible to control behaviour given the right circumstances. Skinner's view is that all behaviour is learned as a result of reinforcement and therefore behaviour can be shaped by controlling the consequences of behaviour. I say jump, you jump and get some form of **reinforcement**, then you are more likely to do it again in the future.

Operant conditioning

In operant conditioning there are different consequences for our behaviour (see Table 7.2).

Table 7.2 Consequences of behaviour in operant conditioning

Consequence	Description
Positive reinforcement	Every time behaviour is appropriate a reward/reinforcer is given, reinforcers can be primary or secondary: primary reinforcer – directly pleasurable rewards such as food; secondary reinforcer – indirectly pleasurable as they can be exchanged for primary reinforcers, e.g. money.
Negative reinforcement	A way of avoiding something negative by behaving in an appropriate way, e.g. cleaning your room to avoid being grounded.
Punishment	Something unpleasant is done because the behaviour was inappropriate, e.g. being told off for talking in class.

Think!

Which of these consequences do you think works best?

Which would work best with criminals? Why?

Interleave me now

Institutionalisation

It isn't easy for most people to understand the psychological effects of prison, particularly the notion of institutionalisation, as they have never experienced it. The complete lack of control in which you must follow the rules absolutely in such a confined environment, combined with having everything done for you and not having to make any decisions for yourself. This was part of the motivation for the Stanford Prison Experiment (SPE).

The Stanford Prison Experiment (SPE)

Zimbardo (1971) conducted an experiment on the psychology of imprisonment (SPE) in which he wanted to see if he could recreate the psychological experience of prison in a group of volunteers with no experience of that kind of institution. He created a fake prison in the basement of the psychology department at Stanford University and then set out to recruit a group of volunteers.

The experiment was designed to last for two weeks with student volunteers playing the roles of both prisoners and guards. However, the experiment only lasted for six days due to the fact that the situation became so unbearable for the volunteer prisoners that Zimbardo was convinced to call it off.

The result of this was greater recognition of the effect that prison can have on those new to the system and the greater recognition needed to see just how the treatment that is given out might affect those involved in the situation. However, it also helped to expose how these situations might affect the guards as they became increasingly uncaring and even brutal towards the prisoners and both sets of volunteers lost perspective on who they really were and became more like what they felt was their role, e.g. like a guard or a prisoner.

Application to everyday life

Prison life in the UK

The psychological effects of being in prison continue to be recognised by the UK government, as seen by a recent report published by Her Majesty's Inspectorate of Prisons (2015) entitled 'The first 24 hours in prison'. In the report, emphasis is placed on the need to recognise the frailty of first-time prisoners and how the treatment by the guards can have a major impact on this. It refers to unnecessary strip searches, the lack of communication with prisoners and a general lack of respect shown by some guards, all of which contributed to the prisoners feeling insecure and that they weren't safe or couldn't cope.

Similar issues were raised about the treatment of prisoners at Abu Ghraib prison in Iraq during the war in Iraq in 2003. US soldiers and reservists had been put in charge of this military prison and were later seen to be behaving in a brutal manner towards the detainees, including stripping them naked and forcing them into degrading acts. Some of the soldiers were prosecuted and went to jail in spite of the fact that one of the witnesses who appeared at their trial was none other than Phil Zimbardo.

AO3 (Analysis and evaluation of knowledge): How useful are these ways of dealing with offending?

Universities of crime

One of the common criticisms of the use of custodial sentencing is that rather than the lesson being learned that you shouldn't commit this crime because you don't want to go back there, i.e. deterrence. All too often, the kind of lessons being learned are how to be more proficient at committing crime or possibly even learning to do new crimes. Prisons may just be places where criminals learn new skills, which can be employed in crime, rather than new skills for a new, non-criminal profession.

One of the problems with sending people to prison is that they are put in a place where the only people they are likely to mix with are other criminals. Sutherland's differential association theory suggests that crime develops because people, particularly young people, mix with individuals who have an alternative set of values to the rest of the population and if you spend enough time with them, you are likely to pick up these values.

Furthermore, Sutherland argues that people also learn the techniques involved in crime in these situations, so it shouldn't be surprising that this also happens to people in prison, particularly as these people will be their role models and it's likely that the worse they are, the more status they are likely to command, which could make them more likely to be followed.

This suggests that prison might be the worst place to put criminals as it will be just the sort of place they could do with avoiding. As Steve Cattell, 'Britain's most prolific criminal' once said, I went into prison as a burglar and I came out a drug dealer (Cattell and Greaves, 2008). Not exactly progress, is it?

Alternatives to custodial sentencing

Some of the alternatives to custodial sentencing are considered in the next chapter, including the use of restorative justice and anger management programmes, each of which have their own value.

Restorative justice works on the basis of trying to include the victim in the process of dealing with offenders by allowing them to make impact statements but also trying to make the offender's make up for their crimes in some way, partially by meeting their victim and apologising but also by giving something back to the community in the form of community service.

Research into the effectiveness of the use of community service as an alternative to custody has received mixed support from Abramovaite et al. (2019), who found that community service was more effective than custody in reducing property crime and theft but not so effective in reducing violent crime and sexual offences.

This suggests that restorative justice has limited effectiveness and is mostly relevant to acquisitive crimes, which involved a system where the payback to the individual or community could be monetised. However, where this isn't possible, as in violent and sexual offences, then its usefulness is significantly more limited. In such cases, anger management may be more applicable.

Rehabilitation or retribution: Which works best?

The figures for recidivism suggest that re-offending is a major problem with most prisons around the world, which brings into question whether putting people in prison actually works. However, a further issue arising from this is whether it is better to have a prison that works by purely punishing prisoners or by attempting to reform them.

The two figures that stand out from Table 7.1 (see p. 91) are Israel at 18 per cent and Norway at 20 per cent. There are conflicting reports from the conditions in Israeli prisons; while it is true that all prisoners can vote, it has also recently been reported (after some unannounced inspections) that prisoners face inhumane conditions in the prisons (Bachner, 2019). However, much more is known about the prison system in Norway, as it is firmly based on the notion of rehabilitation and the idea that if you treat people well and train them, then they can be reformed and go on to live better lives. According to the governor of Bastoey prison near Oslo, the idea is to make the prisons as much like normal life as possible, so prisoners ski, cook, play tennis and even have a beach to go to. This seems to be supported by the figures for recidivism as they are clearly a lot lower than the UK.

However, the claim made against Norway is that they are too soft on their prisoners and visitors to these prisons from the US have described them as being utopian, for the inmates that is. However, a report from the US Crime and Justice Institute has argued that harsh incarcerating can actually increase the rate of recidivism and has suggested that imprisonment and the treatment of prisoners should be targeted towards individual prisoners rather than treating them all the same (US Crime and Justice Institute, 2007).

The ultimate issue seems to be that if you are intending to put people back on the streets when they finish their sentence, you probably need to consider what sort of people you want out there. As Are Hoidel, Halden Prison's director, puts it: 'Every inmate in Norwegian prisons are going back to the society. Do you want people who are angry—or people who are rehabilitated?' (Sterbenz, 2014).

Question time

What do these evaluation points tell us about the use of custodial sentencing?

Is prison the best place for prisoners?

Are there alternatives that could work for all prisoners or just for some?

Can token economies work in prisons?

The use of behaviour modification has been shown to be effective in the treatment of schizophrenia (McMonagle and Sultana 2000) and in changing behaviour in schools (Zlomke and Zlomke 2003). However, it is still questionable to what extent it can be successful in a prison situation with adults who have already shown themselves to be resistant to following rules and who may try to exploit the situation.

A meta-analysis of 26 studies looking at the effectiveness of the use of token economy systems in closed institutions (mostly prisons) was conducted by Gendreau et al. (2014) on behalf of the International Association for Correctional and Forensic Psychology. They wanted to see the effect of such systems on a range of behavioural and educational procedures within these institutions.

The meta-analysis revealed that the systems produced significant improvements in institutional adjustment and educational and work-related behaviours. The systems reduced a wide range of undesirable behaviours by an average of 54 per cent and there were several studies that produced gains much higher than this.

This suggests that token economies are very successful in helping prisoners to adapt to prison life and possibly reducing some of the psychological effects on mental health and suicide but also in improving the possibility of rehabilitation by encouraging prisoners to become involved in educational programmes and possibly learning new skills in a work-based situation.

Problems with behaviour modification

In spite of the apparent success of token economy systems, there are a number of problems with the management of such systems, two of which are: ethical issues in their deployment, particularly questions of informed consent and whether they are abusing prisoners' rights; a problem of training and resources being put into the schemes to ensure they are consistently run.

With regard to ethics, Gendreau et al. (2014) have highlighted the issue of informed consent and the fact that many of these programmes are mandatory, so prisoners have no choice but to be enrolled on them whether they like it or not and may therefore be losing out on important privileges, which may, in other circumstances, be regarded as human rights, e.g. the ability to spend time exercising. This has been further highlighted by a report by Her Majesty's Inspectorate of Prisons, which found that incentive programmes are increasingly becoming more focused on punishment rather than rewards, 'despite evidence pointing to the greater effectiveness of rewards over sanctions, most schemes focused on punitive measures rather than rewarding, encouraging and celebrating positive behaviour' (HMIP, 2018).

With regard to the question of training and resources, Gendreau et al. (2014) have argued that too often institutions suffer from what they call panaceaphilia as they throw themselves into any new initiative that comes along without giving sufficient regard to how it will be financed or the training that would be needed to run it effectively.

This is likely to be a big problem for token economy systems as it has long been established that such systems need consistency in their application if they are to be run effectively and if this doesn't happen, you may end up with the kind of problems referred to in the HMIP (2018) report, which also noted a particular problem with favouritism in the running of these schemes.

Mini plenary

Using the evaluation points above, try to evaluate the following statement:

Custodial sentencing is an ineffective way of dealing with offending behaviour

Arguments for	Arguments against

A modern issue: How can we deal with recidivism?

The problem of recidivism has been explored at length in this chapter but one of the important issues concerns the findings above that for sentences of less than 12 months' duration, the recidivism figure increases to 64.5 per cent. It seems that short custodial sentences are particularly bad.

New research

Reducing the use of short prison sentences in favour of a smarter approach, Revolving Doors agency, 4 February 2019.

In the article, the belief is explained that short sentences for criminals are short-sighted and the government are encouraged to scrap the use of custodial sentences of less than six months. They believe that these should be replaced by a much greater emphasis on community service, particularly involving programmes that address the offender's drug use or mental health problems or both.

They quote government officials who have endorsed this idea and suggest that there has been increasing support for this idea from both the public and the media. According to Lord Keen of Ellie, the government's justice spokesperson in the lords: 'There is persuasive evidence showing that short custodial sentences do not work in terms of rehabilitation and helping offenders turn their backs on crime'.

According to the article, this matters because there is strong evidence that short sentences don't work. Using freedom of information legislation, they found that: three in five report a drug or alcohol problem on arrival at prison; one in four are released homeless; seven in ten reoffend within a year of release. Unfortunately, it is the case that over half the people sent to prison are sent there for six months or less.

The report argues that this approach is short-sighted and offers nothing to the offender in terms of rehabilitation for crimes that are usually not violent so do not require the offender to be removed for public safety reasons. They also argue for a smarter approach, which would be beneficial to both the offender and society as 'putting someone on a community pathway as opposed to a prison pathway would save the criminal justice system £9,237 per person over the course of a year'. This would mean significant savings for society in terms of money but possibly also in terms of reduced offending.

Question time

What does this article tell us about the use of custodial sentencing?

Which type of criminals should prison be used for?

Should there be a total ban on short prison sentences?

Chapter plenary

1. What is meant by custodial sentencing?
2. What are the aims of custodial sentencing?
3. What is the problem of recidivism?
4. What are the psychological effects of custodial sentencing?
5. What is meant by the term institutionalisation?
6. What is behaviour modification?
7. How do token economies work?
8. How does the learning approach apply to the use of custodial sentencing?
9. What does the Stanford Prison Experiment tell us about the use of custodial sentencing?
10. What is meant by the term 'universities of crime'?
11. What are the alternatives to custodial sentencing?
12. Rehabilitation or retribution, which works best?
13. Can token economies work in prisons?
14. What are the problems with behaviour modification?
15. What does new research suggest about how can we deal with recidivism?

Glossary

Key word	Definition
Anger management	A form of cognitive behavioural therapy, which tries to change the thinking patterns of offenders so that they respond to others in a less hostile manner.
Community service	A sentence or order that is given to offenders as an alternative to custodial sentencing, which requires them to do some form of unpaid work to benefit the community.
Differential association theory	Sutherland's theory that offending is caused by learning the attitudes and techniques related to crime from the kind of people you associate with.
Functional skills	The skills needed to function in everyday life, such as reading, writing and basic maths.
Meta-analysis	A method of research using data from a number of previous studies to try to establish an overall trend.
Panaceaphilia	The extremely positive feeling towards any idea or change that is new and aims to be an answer to all problems.
Reinforcement	Anything that increases the likelihood that a response will occur.
Restorative justice	A system that focuses on the rehabilitation of offenders through reconciliation with victims and the community at large.
Token economy system	A system whereby tokens are given for appropriate behaviour that can be exchanged for rewards or privileges.
Utopian	A state in which everything is perfect or ideal.

Plenary: Exam-style questions and answers with advisory comments

Question 1.

Using an example, explain what is involved in behaviour modification for offending. [4 marks]

Marks for this question: AO1 = 4

Advice: In a question like this, it's important to make sure you provide enough detail in the explanation and that you are giving an example, as this has been asked for in the question. There is no need to provide any analysis or evaluation as all of the marks are for AO1: Knowledge and understanding.

Possible answer: According to the Law of Effect, any behaviour that is followed by pleasant consequences is likely to be repeated and therefore the best way to change behaviour is to try to associate the desired behaviour with something pleasant, which is the basic idea behind behaviour modification. Good behaviour on the part of the prisoners will be repeated if it is followed by some kind of reward or privilege.

An example of behaviour modification for offending is the token economy, which works on the basis of operant conditioning in that desirable behaviour can be exchanged for some form of token, which can in turn be exchanged for some form of privilege. In prison, desirable behaviour is likely to be sticking to the rules, staying out of fights and generally doing what you are told. Privileges are likely to come in the form of time out of your cell, being able to wear your own clothes and even having a TV in your cell.

Question 2.

Discuss the use of custodial sentencing and behaviour modification in custody in dealing with offending behaviour. **[16 marks]**

Marks for this question: AO1 = 6 and AO3 = 10

Advice: This question asks you to focus on two topics and as such there is a need to consider the fact that you have to go for breadth rather than depth in your answer as you will need to cut down on the detail to make sure you cover both topics.

This question is looking for both skills of knowledge and understanding, and analysis and evaluation. As there are 6 marks for AO1 and 10 for AO3, there should be greater emphasis on the evaluation. However, all such extended writing questions are marked holistically and therefore it is important that the knowledge is accurate and detailed and that the evaluation is clear and effective.

Possible answer: Across the world, the most common way of dealing with offenders is to make them spend some time in prison. Custodial sentencing is just that, the process whereby, having been found guilty of a crime, someone is removed from the rest of society by being placed in an institution (prison or young offenders' institution).

There are four main aims associated with the use of custodial sentencing; one is retribution, which involves making offenders pay for their crime by being punished harshly and prison is often the harshest punishment some societies have. Another is incapacitation, which involves removing the offender from society so that they can't commit any more crimes and they are no longer a danger to anyone. The third is deterrence and this means using prison as a way of putting offenders off any further crime and making an example of them so that others will see that it's not a good idea to commit crime. The final aim is for the purpose of reformation or rehabilitation and this suggests that prison should be a time when offenders can learn new skills and become better people so that when they go back to society, they won't offend again.

The use of behaviour modification in custody is based on the idea that learned behaviour can be unlearned and therefore offending behaviour can be conditioned while the offender is in prison. According to the Law of Effect, any behaviour that is followed by pleasant consequences is likely to be repeated and therefore the best way to change behaviour is to try to associate the desired behaviour with something pleasant, which is the basic idea behind behaviour modification. Good behaviour on the part of the prisoners will be repeated if it is followed by some kind of reward or privilege.

An example of behaviour modification for offending is the token economy, which works on the basis of operant conditioning in that desirable behaviour can be exchanged for some form of token, which can in turn be exchanged for some form of privilege. In prison, desirable behaviour is likely to be sticking to the rules, staying out of fights and generally doing what you are told. Privileges are likely to come in the form of time out of your cell, being able to wear your own clothes and even having a TV in your cell.

One of the common criticisms of the use of custodial sentencing is that rather than the lesson being learned – that you shouldn't commit this crime because you don't want to go back there, e.g. deterrence – all too often, the kind of lessons being learned are how to be more proficient at committing crime or possibly even learning to do new crimes. Prisons may just be places where criminals learn new skills that can be employed in crime, rather than new skills for a new, non-criminal profession.

One of the problems with sending people to prison is that they are put in a place where the only other people they are likely to mix with are other criminals. Sutherland's differential association theory suggests that crime develops because people, particularly young people, mix with individuals who have an alternative set of values to the rest of the population and if you spend enough time with them, you are likely to pick up these values. This suggests that prison might be the worst place to put criminals as it will be just the sort of place they could do with avoiding.

The figures for recidivism in the UK are that nearly 40 per cent of prisoners re-offend within 12 months, which suggest that re-offending is a major problem with most prisons, which brings into question whether putting people in prison actually works. However, a further issue arising from this is whether it is better to have a prison that works by purely punishing prisoners or by attempting to reform them.

Norway has a prison system that is firmly based on the notion of rehabilitation and the idea that if you treat people well and train them, then they can be reformed and go on to live better lives and their recidivism figures are 20 per cent. According to the governor of Bastoey prison near Oslo, the idea is to make the prisons as much like normal life as possible, so prisoners ski, cook, play tennis and even have a beach to go to. This seems to be supported by the figures for recidivism as they are clearly a lot lower than the UK.

The use of behaviour modification has been shown to be effective in the treatment of schizophrenia. However, it is still questionable to what extent it can be successful in a prison situation with adults who have already shown themselves to be resistant to following rules and who may try to exploit the situation.

A meta-analysis of 26 studies looking at the effectiveness of the use of token economy systems in closed institutions (mostly prisons) was conducted by

Gendreau et al. They revealed that the systems produced significant improvements in institutional adjustment and educational and work-related behaviours. The systems reduced a wide range of undesirable behaviours by an average of 54 per cent and there were several studies that produced gains much higher than this.

This suggests that token economies are very successful in helping prisoners to adapt to prison life and possibly reducing some of the psychological effects on mental health and suicide but also in improving the possibility of rehabilitation by encouraging prisoners to become involved in educational programmes and possibly learning new skills in a work-based situation.

In spite of the apparent success of token economy systems, there are a number of problems with the management of such systems, one of which is the ethical issues in their deployment, particularly questions of informed consent and whether they are abusing prisoners' rights.

Gendreau et al. have highlighted the issue of informed consent and the fact that many of these programmes are mandatory, so prisoners have no choice but to be enrolled on them whether they like it or not and may therefore be losing out on important privileges which may, in other circumstances, be regarded as human rights, e.g. the ability to spend time exercising. This has been further highlighted by a report by Her Majesty's Inspectorate of Prisons, which found that incentive programmes are increasingly becoming more focused on punishment rather than rewards. This brings into question the use of behaviour modification programmes and whether there is much of a future for the whole use of custodial sentencing for offenders.

References

Abramovaite, J., Bandyopadhyay, S., Bhattacharya, S. and Cowen, N. (2019). Alternatives to custody: Evidence from police force areas in England and Wales, *The British Journal of Criminology*, 59(4), July: 800–822.

Bachner, M. (2019). Report finds inhumane treatment of inmates widespread in Israeli prisons, The Israel Times, 12 May, accessed 17 February 2020.

Cattell, S. and Greaves, L. (2008). *Unbreakable*. Milton Keynes: Authentic.

Crime and Justice Institute, Warren, R. (2007). *Evidence-Based Practice to Reduce Recidivism: Implications for State Judiciaries*. Washington, DC: National Institute of Corrections.

Gendreau, P., Listwan, S.J., Kuhns, J.B. and Exum, M.L. (2014). Making prisoners accountable: Are contingency management programs the answer? *Criminal Justice and Behavior*, 41(9): 1079–1102.

Her Majesty's Inspectorate of Prisons (2015). Life in prison: The first 24 hours in prison. London: HMIP.

Her Majesty's Inspectorate of Prisons (2018). Incentivising and promoting good behaviour. London: HMIP.

McMonagle, T. and Sultana, A. (2000). Token economy for schizophrenia. *Cochrane Database of Systematic Reviews*, (3).

Prisons and Probation Ombudsman (2014). Learning from PPO Investigations: Risk factors in self-inflicted deaths in prisons, p. 12.

Skinner, B.F. (1953). *Science and Human Behavior*. Simon and Schuster.

Sterbenz, C. (2014). Why Norway's prison system is so successful. *Business Insider*, 11.

Yukhnenko, D., Sridhar, S. and Fazel, S. (2019). A systematic review of criminal recidivism rates worldwide: 3-year update. *Wellcome Open Research*, 4.

Zimbardo, P.G., Haney, C., Banks, W.C. and Jaffe, D. (1971). *Stanford Prison Experiment*. Zimbardo, Incorporated.

Zlomke, K. and Zlomke, L. (2003). Token economy plus self-monitoring to reduce disruptive classroom behaviors. *The Behavior Analyst Today*, 4(2): 177.

Chapter 8
Dealing with offending behaviour 2 – Restorative justice and anger management

Dealing with offending behaviour: anger management; restorative justice.

AO1 (Knowledge and understanding): Dealing with offending behaviour 2 – Restorative justice and anger management

What is anger management?

In Chapter 5, the application of cognitive factors for explaining crime was put forward in the form of cognitive behavioural therapy (CBT), which aims to combine trying to deal with the faulty thinking that might lead someone into a hostile attribution bias, for example, as well as trying to deal with the behaviour that may follow such irrational thoughts.

One form of CBT that is specifically designed to deal with this kind of problem in a criminal setting is anger management, which attempts to deal with the negative thoughts and behaviour that arise from faulty cognition and then replace that with more appropriate thoughts and behaviour.

Stages of anger management

1. **Cognitive preparation**

   The therapist would talk through the situations that the individual finds anger provoking and the pattern that their particular thoughts and behaviour would go through when faced with these situations. The offender would be asked to keep a diary of their experiences, which would hopefully help them to develop the ability to recognise when they were going to become angry. They would also be asked to recognise the feelings that would accompany these thoughts so that they would have the potential to change their level of arousal by some form of relaxation technique. This is encouraged as it is based on the belief that it isn't possible to feel angry and relaxed at the same time.

2. **Skill acquisition and rehearsal**

   The focus in this stage is on the offender learning the skills that will prevent them from simply reacting to their aroused state by lashing out or attacking someone. One important skill in this process is learning to use self-talk as a way of taking control of their arousal with a package of statements that could be used in anger-provoking situations. These statements encourage the offender to remain problem-focused so that they are focusing on the solution to the problem rather than their feeling of arousal, which should divert their attention from those feelings. Alongside this, the offender would be taught practical skills, such as tensing and relaxing their muscles one at a time and using breathing techniques to encourage relaxation. They would then be encouraged to practice these skills before applying them in the real world.

3. **Practice and application**

   The offender would be encouraged to practice their new skills in a series of situations that would gradually become more provocative, based on a hierarchy that would have been previously prepared by the offender themselves. These situations could be taken from their anger diaries and involve the use of some of the statements that they had prepared in the previous stage. The application of the skills learned in the previous stage would then be used in imagined, role-played and finally, direct conditions. This would allow for the offender to change their behaviour in real situations while at the same time teaching them to develop a whole new set of feelings involving empathy and compassion.

Question time

Why does the offender need to be able to recognise situations that are likely to make them become angry?

What sort of skills will they need to learn to use when they notice these situations?

Why do they use role-play to practice the use of these new skills?

What is restorative justice?

The use of restorative justice has already been discussed to some extent in Chapter 7 as part of the alternative to custodial sentencing. Restorative justice is based on the notion of community service, which has existed in some form since the 1970s in the UK. The idea of community service is that it should be 'practical, rehabilitative and functional' (Bergman, 1975), in that it would be less costly, involve the offender giving back something to society and also create real communication between the offender and the rest of society. These principles have been developed further in the use of restorative justice.

General principles of restorative justice

According to the legal guidance given by the Crown Prosecution Service (2017, updated 2019), restorative justice should have the following aims:

- *Victim satisfaction* – to reduce the fear felt by the victim and to create a feeling that they have been paid back for the harm done to them.
- *Engagement with the perpetrator* – to make the offender aware of the damage they have done and to agree to do something to make up for it.
- *Creation of community capital* – so that the public can see that something constructive is being done and become more confident in the system of justice.

Main features of restorative justice

Meeting – offender and victim have the chance to meet face-to-face so that the victim can explain how they have been affected by the crime.

Responsibility – the offender must admit to their crime and be prepared to make up for it in some way.

Active – rather than being a passive process in which the offender is just given a sentence, it should be active as it involves the offender doing something to make up for their crime.

Positive – as it opens up a way forward for both the victim, who is now heard and their needs recognised, and the offender, who can now feel like they have done something practical rather than just having something done to them.

Flexibility – rather than operating on rigid principles of one type of punishment fits all, this recognises the need to use a different approach for each crime and to make the punishment fit the crime.

The Restorative Justice Council (RJC) – is an independent body set up to offer advice and guidance for those in need of justice and for those delivering it to ensure that the general principles are met.

Think!

Why is it important that the victim is involved in this process?

Why does the offender need to take responsibility for their crime?

Is this a way forward for all forms of crime?

Mini plenary

Without referring back to the text, identify the main features/stages of anger management and restorative justice.

	Anger management	Restorative justice
Main features		

AO2 (Application of knowledge): How does this apply in practice?

Interleave me now

The cognitive approach – assumptions

- The study of cognitive processes is important in understanding behaviour.
- Cognitive processes mediate between stimulus and response.
- Thoughts influence behaviour.
- Humans actively process information.

Schemas and offending behaviour

Schemas are mental representations of some aspect of our world; they are packets of related ideas that we develop through experience. Each time we have a new experience, we build on our schema so that we build up a complete picture about what happens in certain situations. We also have a tendency towards a confirmatory bias so that we only focus on those things that go the way we expect and ignore the things that don't, so if we have encountered people behaving aggressively towards us in the past, then we might be on the lookout for that behaviour again in the future.

An example that is relevant to offending behaviour would be what happens in situations where we are trying to understand the behaviour of people we are coming into contact with for the first time, e.g. at the pub. Based on experiences from the past, we might have a schema that says people might try to challenge us and so our initial response is to be aggressive to prevent this from happening, but of course this behaviour might make it more likely to happen and so it continues as part of a 'vicious' circle.

Think!

Do you think it's possible to change your behaviour by changing the way you think?

Can you think yourself out of being angry?

Is it possible to create new schemas that will change your behaviour?

Mini plenary

Jane has been offered the opportunity to take part in a programme of anger management as part of her probation for violent offences. She has been told that she needs to deal with the way that she sees other people's behaviour and the way that she reacts in certain situations. She has also been told that she will learn new behaviour that she could use in these situations.

With reference to what Jane is going to be doing, explain what is involved in anger management.

_____

_____

_____

_____

_____

_____

_____

_____

AO3 (Analysis and evaluation of knowledge): How useful are these ways of dealing with offending?

The benefits of anger management

The benefits of anger management can be at least partially judged in comparison to other therapeutic approaches, such as behaviour modification. The theory behind each approach is somewhat different and may give an indication of the likely success.

While behaviour modification is based on an approach that attempts to simply change behaviour, which may only last as long as the therapy is being employed, anger management is based on changing the thinking behind the behaviour as well as the behaviour, as such it may be possible for it to be employed beyond the period in which the therapy is being conducted.

According to Walters (2014), the integration of cognitive and behavioural skills makes the use of CBT (anger management) with offenders much more beneficial in the long term. This is particularly true as the procedures learned and perfected in the therapeutic environment are then transferred to the real life of the offender. Walters further argues that a part of the reason that anger management is sometimes not successful is because it fails to provide a proper follow-up process. He encourages those in therapy to reattend therapeutic sessions in which they can talk to the therapist about their progress and, if need be, the therapist can work to reinforce the skills previously learned.

One of the particularly important parts of the process is the feeling of empowerment that can be gained. Walters uses the example of an offender called Fred who was part of a progamme and during the follow up the therapist was able to pick up on something that hadn't been noticed before, which was that Fred had been suffering from a central auditory processing deficit from birth that made it difficult for him to control his angry feelings. The therapist was able to work on this at the same time as the normal CBT procedures, which became empowering for him and he was able to stay away from offending.

This particularly supports the cognitive aspects of anger management as it combines the mental processes with a neurological understanding that is one of the features of cognitive neuroscience.

What are the problems with anger management?

There are a couple of issues with anger management worth mentioning, which are that it may not be effective in the long term and it can be expensive and require a lot of commitment on the part of the offender. These issues might mean that its effectiveness is limited.

A meta-analysis of 58 studies by Lipsey et al. (2007) found that the likelihood of not reoffending in the 12 months after intervention for individuals in the treatment group was 1.53 times as great as those for individuals in the control group; this represents a 25 per cent decrease. However, neither this study or many others have been able to successfully show the long-term effectiveness and so it is hard to draw conclusions about this from the information currently available.

One study that has attempted to look at long-term effectiveness was a longitudinal investigation of the effectiveness of cognitive-behavioural treatment with sexual offenders, which compared a group of offenders treated with an anger management programme, with two untreated prison control groups and found that there were no significant differences among the three groups in their rates of sexual or violent reoffending over an eight-year follow-up period.

This brings into question the usefulness of such programmes and may also point to the other problem, which relates to the lack of commitment to the programme. It may be that offenders are taking part in the programme as they feel that it will provide them with more lenient treatment, but in the long term they do not maintain that commitment and return to their old ways.

How effective is restorative justice?

The ultimate test of any system is how effective it is in changing the behaviour of those that are subjected to it. If we are going to judge the effectiveness of restorative justice then we could look at how punitive these systems are in terms of constituting a real punishment and their effect on recidivism.

According to Robert Kaye from the policy exchange think tank, the use of restorative justice in the form of community payback isn't working, because many of the orders associated with this process are for no more than one year and even then, nearly half of these orders weren't successfully completed in 2009. They weren't successfully completed, because the offender committed another crime before they were finished, with over a quarter of a million crimes being committed by those with such orders within 12 months and with 1,500 of these involving serious crimes such as rape and murder.

Kaye goes on to argue that the 'payback' involved in these cases was often not hard enough, with most tasks involving things that community volunteers would normally do such as hedge trimming and that many were only for 18 hours a week, even for those convicted of knife crimes.

However, using different criteria, Strang et al. (2013) found the effect on victims of restorative justice was more successful and that overall, victims who had experienced restorative justice were more satisfied with the outcome than those who had been victims in cases that involved normal methods of criminal justice processing. Other studies have found similar levels of victim satisfaction with restorative justice. Shapland et al. (2007) found that about 85 per cent of victims (and 80 per cent of offenders) were satisfied with their experience. In particular, only 12 per cent of victims (and 10 per cent of offenders) expressed any doubt about the outcome agreement reached at the end of the process, and almost all thought it was fair.

This suggests that the effectiveness of restorative justice may depend on how it is being judged and that if judged specifically in terms of recidivism, it may not work, particularly with violent offenders but if judged from the point of view of the victim then it may be that it is a lot more satisfying than custodial sentencing alone.

Are these approaches relevant to all crimes?

One of the problems considered in Chapter 7 was concerned with the useful-ness of alternative programmes for crimes such as domestic violence. It has been argued that the suggestion that domestic violence is about anger is wrong as it is actually about control and that it can't therefore be successfully treated by using this approach Maietta (2014). This can be seen quite clearly because the abuser doesn't go around attacking anyone, just their intimate partner; to everyone else they can seem perfectly normal with no tendency to anger at all. Furthermore, Jo (2012) argues that domestic abusers may still be prepared to go down this road as it carries less stigma than going to sessions that are specifically for such abusers.

One of the issues identified by Kaye (2010) for the use of restorative justice is the question of whether it is being used for the right offences. Kaye found that there was increasing use of the system with violent offenders and those that had committed knife crimes, for whom the system may literally have no chance of working. The system of restoring something might only work for those offences where there can be some clear payback for the victim or community. This may, therefore, only be relevant for crimes of theft or property damage whereby the notion of payback is much easier to quantify.

It seems that attempting to use some of these alternative approaches for crimes where they simply don't fit is doomed to failure. Therefore, it may be difficult to judge their success or otherwise unless they are used in places where there is a clear potential benefit, i.e. anger management used for crimes that involve actual uncon-trolled anger (as many crimes do not) and restorative justice for crimes where there is clearly likely to be something that can be restored or some form of meaningful payback provided.

Think!

What do these evaluation points tell us about the usefulness of anger management and restorative justice?

Are they best used separately or would it be better to have a combined approach to the treatment of offenders?

Can they be a real alternative to the use of custodial sentencing?

Mini plenary

Using the evaluation points above, try to evaluate the following statement:

Anger management and restorative justice are both effective ways of dealing with offending behaviour.

Arguments for	Arguments against

A modern issue: Do offenders see community service as a soft option?

The media often present the use of restorative justice and community service as a soft option with some newspapers claiming that this isn't just the view of the public but the view of offenders too. In order to test this, a couple of researchers decided to systematically question offenders about their experiences of different types of punishment.

New research

Esther F.J.C. van Ginneken, Leiden University, The Netherlands, and David Hayes, University of Sheffield, UK, (2017). 'Just' punishment? Offenders' views on the meaning and severity of punishment, Criminology & Criminal Justice.

In this research, van Ginneken and Hayes wanted to explore offenders' perception of punishment and how this impacted on their current and future behaviour. They conducted two studies with offenders undergoing the use of incarceration as a punishment and those being subjected to community service. They used the data from these studies to judge how effective the offenders themselves judged these two types of punishment to be.

The researchers used semi-structured interviews with fifteen male and fifteen female prisoners from a category B prison who had a sentence of six months or longer and were within three months of being released. They did the same with seven male and two female offenders from a probation trust who had experienced at least two months of a probation order.

The prison group had mixed views on the effectiveness of being put in prison, with some arguing that it was the only way to deal with crime as deprivation of liberty was pretty bad and others arguing that prison was too easy and the punishment needed to be harder. For example, one prisoner said, 'This is meant to be a punishment. It's not, it's a joke. People have got better lives in here than they have on road. Here, you get everything for free and that. You get your dinner for free, you get clean clothes. Why do you think I keep coming in jail? Because I know, jail is a joke'.

Similarly, some of the community service group saw it as a real punishment, as they felt that someone else controlled their lives and they were subjected to humiliation and feelings of guilt and embarrassment. However, others didn't feel that it was much of a punishment, 'Cause coming in to probation, to me, is not punishment. It's like me going to the doctor's, once a fortnight. Similar type of thing to me'.

The issue of 'payback' was quite important for some of the probationers as they believed that if you weren't made to do something to pay back then it wasn't a real punishment, 'I was charged with fraud. For me to attend here every fortnight is not a punishment. It is not a punishment. I should have been made to have paid at least some of that money back. Then that would have been more of a punishment than this'.

On the whole, there were very different views coming from each of the two groups and it often seemed like a very personal matter, with some focusing on the unintended consequences of going to prison, such as not being able to get a job afterwards and others focusing on the idea that prison was easy as you could do it and then get out and start your life again and that probation and community service was more of a hardship than prison.

Question time

What does this article tell us about the use of community service?

Can programmes like this be used for everyone? How can we know who to use them for and who not to use them for?

Should we be taking a more individual approach to dealing with offenders? What are the problems with doing that?

1. What is anger management?
2. What are the stages of anger management?
3. What is restorative justice?
4. What are the general principles behind restorative justice?
5. What are the main features of restorative justice?
6. What are the assumptions of the cognitive approach?
7. How do schemas relate to offending behaviour?
8. What are the benefits of anger management?
9. What are the problems with anger management?
10. How effective is restorative justice?
11. Are anger management and restorative justice relevant to all crimes?
12. Do offenders themselves see community service as a soft option?

Glossary

Key word	Definition
Behaviour modification	A way of changing undesirable behaviour by associating it with positive or negative consequences.
Central auditory processing deficit	The inability to process incoming information in the way that others do, particularly in relation to hearing.
Cognitive behavioural therapy (CBT)	A talking therapy that can help you manage your problems by changing the way you think and behave.
Community service	A sentence or order that is given to offenders, as an alternative to custodial sentencing, which requires them to do some form of unpaid work to benefit the community.
Empowerment	The process of becoming more confident to be able to deal with your own difficulties, rather than leaving it to someone else.
Meta-analysis	A method of research using data from a number of previous studies to try to establish an overall trend.
Recidivism	The tendency of a convicted criminal to reoffend.
Vicious circle	A chain of events in which the resolution of one problem causes another problem to occur and so the chain continues.

Plenary: Exam-style questions and answers with advisory comments

Question 1.

Outline how restorative justice has been used with offenders.   **[4 marks]**

Marks for this question: AO1 = 4

Advice: In a question like this, it's important to make sure you are outlining the main features as there is no requirement to go into too much detail. There is no need to provide any analysis or evaluation as all of the marks are for AO1: Knowledge and understanding.

Possible answer: There are a number of important features of restorative justice programmes, which generally include: the offender and victim have the chance to meet face-to-face so that the victim can explain how they have been affected by the crime. The offender must admit to their crime, take responsibility and be prepared to make up for it in some way. Rather than being a passive process, in which the offender is just given a sentence, it should be active as it involves the offender doing something to make up for their crime.

It should also be flexible, rather than operating on rigid principles of one type of punishment fits all. This recognises the need to use a different approach for each crime and to make the punishment fit the crime. Finally, it needs to be positive, rather than negative, so it can be seen as a move in the right direction with the offender doing something to move forwards rather than looking back.

Question 2.

Discuss the use of anger management and restorative justice as ways of dealing with offender behaviour.   **[16 marks]**

Marks for this question: AO1 = 6 and AO3 = 10

Advice: This question asks you to focus on two topics and as such there is a need to consider the fact that you have to go for breadth rather than depth in your answer as you will need to cut down on the detail to make sure you cover both topics.

This question is looking for both skills of knowledge and understanding, and analysis and evaluation. As there are 6 marks for AO1 and 10 for AO3, there should be greater emphasis on the evaluation. However, all such extended writing questions are marked holistically and therefore it is important that the knowledge is accurate and detailed and that the evaluation is clear and effective.

Possible answer: Anger management is a form of cognitive behavioural therapy that attempts to deal with the negative thoughts and behaviour that arise from faulty cognition and then replace that with more appropriate thoughts and behaviour. There are three stages of anger management.

The first stage is cognitive preparation in which the therapist would talk through the situations that the individual finds anger provoking and the pattern that their particular thoughts and behaviour would go through when faced with these situations.

The second stage is skill acquisition and rehearsal in which the focus is on the offender learning the skills that will prevent them from simply attacking someone. One important skill in this process is learning to use self-talk as a way of taking control that could be used in anger-provoking situations. They might also learn relaxation techniques, which they could use when faced with anger-provoking situations.

The third stage is practice and application in which the offender would be encouraged to practice their new skills in a series of situations that would gradually become more provocative based on a hierarchy that would have been previously prepared by the offender themselves. This would allow for the offender to change their behaviour in real situations.

Restorative justice is based on the notion of community service that has existed in some form since the 1970s in the UK. The idea of community service is that it should be practical, rehabilitative and functional, in that it would be less costly, involving the offender giving back something to society and also create real communication between the offender and the rest of society. These principles have been developed further in the use of restorative justice.

Restorative justice should have the following aims: reducing the fear felt by the victim and to create a feeling that they have been paid back for the harm done to them; making the offender aware of the damage they have done and for the offender to agree to do something to make up for it; and the creation of community capital so that the public can see that something constructive is being done and become more confident in the system of justice.

According to Walters, the integration of cognitive and behavioural skills makes the use of anger management with offenders much more beneficial in the long term. This is particularly true as the procedures learned and perfected in the therapeutic environment are then transferred to the real life of the offender. Walters further argues that a part of the reason that anger management is sometimes not successful is because it fails to provide a proper follow-up process. He encourages those in therapy to reattend therapeutic sessions in which they can talk to the therapist about their progress and, if need be, the therapist can work to reinforce the skills previously learned. One of the particularly important parts of the process is the feeling of empowerment that can be gained.

There are a couple of issues with anger management worth mentioning, which are that it may not be effective in the long term and it can be expensive and require a lot of commitment on the part of the offender. These issues might mean that its effectiveness is limited.

A meta-analysis of 58 studies by Lipsey et al. found that the likelihood of not reoffending in the 12 months after intervention for individuals in the treatment group was 1.53 times as great as those for individuals in the control group; this represents a 25 per cent decrease. However, it's difficult to see the long-term effectiveness. One study that attempted to look at long-term effectiveness was a longitudinal investigation of the effectiveness of cognitive-behavioural treatment with sexual offenders, which compared a group of offenders treated with an anger management programme, with two untreated prison control groups and found that there were no significant differences among the three groups in their rates of sexual or violent reoffending over an eight-year follow-up period. This brings into question the usefulness of such programmes.

The ultimate test of any system is how effective it is in changing the behaviour of those that are subjected to it. If we are going to judge the effectiveness of restorative justice then we could look at how punitive these systems are in terms of constituting a real punishment and their effect on recidivism.

According to Robert Kaye from the Policy Exchange think tank, the use of restorative justice in the form of community payback isn't working because many of the orders associated with this process are for no more than one year and even then, nearly half these orders weren't successfully completed in 2009. They weren't successfully completed, because the offender committed another crime before they were finished, with over a quarter of a million crimes being committed by those with such orders within 12 months and with 1,500 of these involving serious crimes such as rape and murder.

Restorative justice and other forms of community service can sometimes be seen as a soft option, so to investigate this van Ginneken looked at the attitude of offenders and found some of the community service group saw it as a real punishment, as they felt that someone else controlled their lives and they were subjected to humiliation and feelings of guilt and embarrassment. However, others didn't feel that it was much of a punishment.

This brings into question any punishment that isn't seen as harsh enough because that could be the very problem that lies at the heart of dealing with crime.

References

Bergman, H.S. (1975). Community service in England: An alternative to custodial sentence. *Fed. Probation*, 39: 43.

Crown Prosecution Service (2017). Restorative Justice: *Legal Guidance*. Reviewed and updated: 24 September 2019, GOV.UK (accessed 17 February 2020).

Jo, K. (5 January 2012). Anger management classes likely to increase domestic abuse, *HealthyPlace*. Retrieved on 19 February 2020, from www.healthyplace.com/blogs/verbalabuseinrelationships/2012/01/anger-management-likely-to-increase-domestic-abuse.

Kaye, R. (2010). Fitting the crime. Reforming community sentences: Mending the weak link in the sentencing chain. www.policyexchange.org.uk/wp-content/uploads/2016/09/fitting-the-crime-nov-10.pdf (accessed 18 February 2020).

Lipsey, M.W., Landenberger, N.A. and Wilson, S.J. (2007). Effects of cognitive-behavioral programs for criminal offenders. *Campbell Systematic Reviews*, 3(1): 1–27.

Maietta, K. (2014). Domestic abuse is not an anger management problem. *Bangor Daily News*, 8 August.

Shapland, J., Atkinson, A., Atkinson, H., Chapman, B., Dignan, J., Howes, M., Johnstone, J., Robinson, G. and Sorsby, A. (2007). Restorative justice: The views of victims and offenders. *Ministry of Justice Research Series*, 3(07).

Strang, H., Sherman, L.W., Mayo-Wilson, E., Woods, D. and Ariel, B. (2013). Restorative justice conferencing (RJC) using face-to-face meetings of offenders and victims: Effects on offender recidivism and victim satisfaction. A systematic review. *Campbell Systematic Reviews*, 9(1): 1–59.

van Ginneken, E.F. and Hayes, D. (2017). 'Just' punishment? Offenders' views on the meaning and severity of punishment. *Criminology & Criminal Justice*, 17(1): 62–78.

Walters, G.D. (2014). Applying CBT to the criminal thought process. Forensic CBT: A handbook for clinical practice, pp. 104–121.

Index

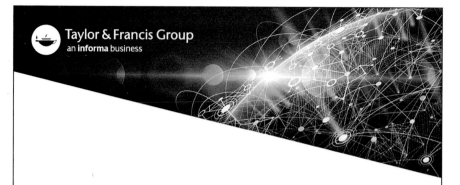